Communion of Churches and Petrine Ministry

Communion of Churches and Petrine Ministry

Lutheran-Catholic Convergences

Group of Farfa Sabina

Translated by Paul Misner

WILLIAM B. EERDMANS PUBLISHING COMPANY

GRAND RAPIDS, MICHIGAN / CAMBRIDGE, U.K.

This volume is a translation of

Gruppe von Farfa Sabina, *Gemeinschaft der Kirchen und Petrusamt: Lutherisch-katholische Annäherungen* (Frankfurt am Main: Verlag Otto Lembeck, 2010).

Published 2014 by
Wm. B. Eerdmans Publishing Co.
2140 Oak Industrial Drive N.E., Grand Rapids, Michigan 49505 /
P.O. Box 163, Cambridge CB3 9PU U.K.

Printed in the United States of America

20 19 18 17 16 15 14   7 6 5 4 3 2 1

Library of Congress Cataloging-in-Publication Data

Gemeinschaft der Kirchen und Petrusamt. English
    Communion of churches and Petrine ministry: Lutheran-Catholic convergences /
    Group of Farfa Sabina ; translated by Paul Misner.
        pages   cm
    Includes bibliographical references.
    ISBN 978-0-8028-7194-7 (pbk.: alk. paper)
    1. Petrine office.   2. Papacy.   3. Lutheran Church — Relations — Catholic Church.
    4. Gruppe von Farfa Sabina.   I. Gruppe von Farfa Sabina.   II. Title.

    BV601.57.G45   2014
    280'.042   dc23

                                                    2014031234

www.eerdmans.com

Contents

Foreword   viii

Abbreviations   x

Introduction   1

I. Luther's Critique of Pope and Papacy and the Roman Reaction   9

   A. Holy Scripture, Tradition, and Teaching Office   10

      1. Luther's Appeal to Holy Scripture and His Critique of the Teaching Office   10

      2. The Roman Reaction in the Sixteenth and in the Following Centuries   15

   B. The Papacy   20

      1. The Multilayered Judgment on Papal Ministry in the Lutheran Reformation   20

      2. Developments in Catholic Understanding of the Papal Ministry   27

II. Vatican I on Papacy (*Pastor Aeternus*)   31

   A. The Infallible Teaching Office of the Pope   31

      1. The Dogma   31

      2. Hermeneutics of the Dogma   32

Contents

3. The Content of the Dogma   32

4. Did the Council Teach an Absolute, Personal,
   and Separate Infallibility of the Pope?   36

5. The Dogma in the Second Vatican Council   40

B. The Universal Jurisdiction of the Pope   43

1. The Universal Jurisdiction of the Pope — Content and
   Qualifications   44

2. Completing and Rebalancing Vatican I   49

3. Vatican I at Vatican II   50

C. A Lutheran Response to the Interpretations of *Pastor
   Aeternus*   52

D. Primacy of Doctrine and Jurisdiction — Necessary?
   An Ecumenical Reflection   55

III. **Confessional Approaches to the *communio ecclesiarum*
     and the Service of Unity**   58

A. *Communio ecclesiarum* and the Service of Unity
   in the Lutheran Churches   58

1. Communio ecclesiarum — *Inner-Lutheran Communion*   60

2. Communio ecclesiarum *Worldwide*   62

B. *Communio ecclesiarum* and Service to Unity
   in the Roman Catholic Church   65

1. Ecclesiological Guidelines of the Second Vatican Council   65

2. The Role of Doctrine in Canonical Norms   68

   Excursus: On the Authority and Binding Character of
   Roman Catholic Magisterial Texts and Curial Documents   74

3. Primacy of Jurisdiction in Contemporary Roman Catholic
   Canon Law   76

4. Theological Considerations   81

C. Appendix: Honorary Primacy in the Early Church and
   communio ecclesiarum — Brief Survey   84

1. The Honorary Primacy in the Early Church   85

2. Orthodox Churches   86

3. Anglican Communion   89

4. Methodist Churches   91

IV. **Promising Developments and Challenges** 93

    A. Promising Developments 94

        1. *Montreal 1963: A New Approach to the Concept of Tradition* 94

        2. *The Second Vatican Council:* Dei verbum *and* Lumen gentium 95

        3. *Lutheran-Catholic Theological Dialogue* 100

3.1. The First International Lutheran-Catholic Dialogue 100

3.2. The Lutheran-Catholic Dialogue in the USA 101

3.3. The Dialogue in Germany between the DBK and the VELKD 103

3.4. The International Lutheran-Catholic Dialogue on Apostolicity 108

    B. Problematic Developments 110

        1. *The Controversy over the Ecclesiological Status of Lutheran Churches* 110

        2. *Lutheranism and the Catholicity of the Church* 113

V. *Ut unum sint:* **Toward a Renewal of the Petrine Ministry** 115

    A. Hermeneutical Principles for the Rereading of Vatican I (Summary) 115

    B. Conclusions and Implications 120

        1. *New Assessments* 120

            1.1. New Evaluation of the Papal Ministry by the Lutheran Churches 120

            1.2. The Roman Catholic Church and the *communio ecclesiarum* 120

            1.3. Consequences 121

        2. *On the Way to a Common Understanding of the Petrine Ministry* 121

            2.1. Petrine Ministry and Council 121

            2.2. Ministry of Unity and Pastoral Leadership or Oversight 123

            2.3. Petrine Ministry in Service of Truth 123

        Members of the Group of Farfa Sabina 126

Foreword

With the presentation of this dialogue report, the Lutheran-Catholic Group of Farfa Sabina has reached the goal of its five-year study project on *Communion of Churches and Petrine Ministry.* In his encyclical *Ut unum sint* of 1995, the late Pope John Paul II raised the question of "the forms in which this ministry" of the successor of Peter in the service of church unity "may accomplish a service of love recognized by all concerned" (no. 95). He went on to appeal to leaders and theologians of the churches "to engage with [him] in a patient and fraternal dialogue on this subject" (no. 96). In response to this invitation, the academic advisory board of the International Bridgettine Centre in Farfa Sabina took the initiative to convoke two symposia on the Petrine Ministry in 2003 and 2004 (see Introduction, footnote 3). These two conferences revealed a decided readiness on the part of all participants (Catholic as well as Lutheran) to scrutinize their respective traditions in the light of biblical and historical research, with the aim of possibly coming to a shared understanding of a universal ministry or office for unity. The positive results of both symposia encouraged the academic advisory board to recommend a permanent dialogue on the Petrine Ministry and its significance for Catholic-Lutheran communion. Accordingly it was decided to create a *Permanent Working Group on the Petrine Ministry* consisting of seven Catholics and seven Lutherans from Germany, France, Italy, and Scandinavia with a commission for five years. The dialogue of the Group of Farfa Sabina owes its existence to a private initiative, yet not without connection to official conversations as sponsored by the Vatican Council for Promoting Christian Unity and the Lutheran World Federation. The aim in view is to pave the road to a rapprochement between the Christian confessions in an area that increasingly proves to be theologically and ecclesially crucial and at the same time poses an impediment to Christian unity.

It is our sincere wish at the conclusion of our work to express our profound thanks above all to the *Fondazione di Farfa* and its president, the abbess general of the Bridgettine Order, Mother Tekla Famiglietti, for her unceasing interest and generous financial aid that made it possible for the Working Group to fulfill its commission. We gratefully recall also the cordial hospitality and the practical assistance rendered to us by the Sisters in the convents of Camaldoli/Naples and Farfa Sabina, where the Group held its plenary sessions. We likewise are most grateful to the Sisters of the Bridgettine convent in Bremen, where the greater part of the editorial work took place. The Sisters of the Bridgettine convent in Maribo, Denmark, kindly hosted the small group that undertook the necessary preparatory work for the English translation (American documentation style in the footnotes, adoption of official English translations of Latin, and German works cited, etc.).

For the painstaking work of translation from the German into English, we are very grateful to Prof. Paul Misner (Milwaukee, Wisconsin). This translation was made possible with the help of an additional donation from the Centro Pro Unione, an Ecumenical Research Center in Rome — a ministry of the Franciscan Friars of the Atonement. We also owe many thanks to Bente Guldsborg (Copenhagen) and Johannes Brosseder* (Königswinter) for their invaluable assistance in the preparation of the English edition of this volume.

In view of the abundance of literature on the papacy and the Petrine office, we have foregone a bibliography at the end of the volume and limited ourselves to citing indispensable scholarly studies in the footnotes.

Rome and Copenhagen, March 2013

<table>
<tr><td>JAMES F. PUGLISI, SA
Catholic Co-Chair</td><td>PEDER NØRGAARD-HØJEN
Lutheran Co-Chair</td></tr>
</table>

**Professor Johannes Brosseder did not live long enough to see the English version of the Farfa Report, toward the publication of which he had invested so much love, energy, and skill. He died in the summer of 2014. This unexepected event occasions us all the more to express our deep appreciation to an extremely dedicated and committed colleague and keep him in precious and grateful memory.*

Abbreviations

AAS	*Acta Apostolicae Sedis*. Città del Vaticano 1909ff.
Antonianum	Periodicum philosophico-theologicum trimestre, Rome
ARCIC	Anglican–Roman Catholic International Commission
BC	*The Book of Concord: The Confessions of the Evangelical Lutheran Church*. Edited by Robert Kolb and Timothy J. Wengert. Minneapolis: Fortress Press, 2000
BSLK	*Die Bekenntnisschriften der evangelisch-lutherischen Kirche*. 12th ed. Göttingen: Vandenhoeck & Ruprecht, 1998
CA	Confessio Augustana
CD	Vaticanum II, *Christus Dominus*. Decretum de pastorali episcoporum munere in Ecclesia
CIC	Codex Iuris Canonici
DBK	Deutsche Bischofskonferenz
DH	Denzinger, Heinrich. *Kompendium der Glaubensbekenntnisse und kirchlichen Lehrentscheidungen*. 40th ed. Edited by Peter Hünermann. Freiburg, Basel, Vienna: Herder, 2005
DV	Vaticanum II, *Dei verbum*. Constitutio dogmatica de divina revelatione
DwÜ	*Dokumente wachsender Übereinstimmung*, vol. 1: 2nd ed. 1931-1982; vol 2: 1982-1990; vol. 3: 1990-2001. Edited by Harding Meyer et al. Paderborn: Bonifatius / Frankfurt am Main: Verlag Otto Lembeck, 1991-2003
ET	English translation
GiA	*Growth in Agreement: Reports and Agreed Statements of Ecumenical Conversations on a World Level* (vol. 1). Edited by Harding Meyer and Lukas Vischer. New York: Paulist Press /

	Geneva: World Council of Churches, 1984; vol. 2, *Reports and Agreed Statements of Ecumenical Conversations on a World Level, 1982-1998*. Edited by Jeffrey Gros, Harding Meyer, and William G. Rusch. Geneva: WCC Publications / Grand Rapids: Eerdmans, 2000; vol. 3: *Growth in Agreement: International Dialogue Texts and Agreed Statements, 1998-2005*. Edited by Jeffrey Gros, Thomas F. Best, and Lorelei F. Fuchs. Geneva: WCC Publications / Grand Rapids: Eerdmans, 2007
GS	Vaticanum II, *Gaudium et spes*. Constitutio pastoralis de Ecclesia in mundo huius temporis
LG	Vaticanum II, *Lumen gentium*. Constitutio dogmatica de Ecclesia
LThK	Lexikon für Theologie und Kirche. 10 vols. and 3 suppl. vols. 2nd ed. Freiburg, Basel, Vienna: Herder, 1957-1967; 3rd. ed. 11 vols. Freiburg, Basel, Vienna: Herder, 1993-2001
LWB	Lutherischer Weltbund
LWF	Lutheran World Federation
Mansi	Sanctorum conciliorum et decretorum collectio nova
ND	Josef Neuner and Jacques Dupuis, eds., *The Christian Faith in the Doctrinal Documents of the Catholic Church*. 7th rev. and enlarged ed. Bangalore: Theological Publ. in India / New York: Alba House, 2001
NRSV	New Revised Standard Version
ÖRK	Ökumenischer Rat der Kirchen
SC	Vaticanum II, *Sacrosanctum Concilium*. Constitutio de sacra liturgia
RSPhTh	Revue des sciences philosophiques et théologiques, Paris
STh	Thomas of Aquino, Summa Theologiae
TRE	*Theologische Realenzyklopädie*, 36 vols. Berlin et al.: W. de Gruyter, 1977-2004; 2 vols. indices. Berlin et al.: W. de Gruyter, 2006-2007
UR	Vatican II, *Unitatis redintegratio*. Decretum de oecumenismo
UUS	Encyclical Letter *Ut unum sint* of Pope John Paul II
VCII	*Vatican Council II: The Basic Sixteen Documents*. Gen. ed., Austin Flannery. Northport, NY: Costello / Dublin: Dominican Publications, 1996
VELKD	Vereinigte Evangelisch-Lutherische Kirche Deutschlands
WA	D. Martin Luthers Werke. Kritische Gesamtausgabe, Weimar: Hermann Böhlau, 1883ff. [Weimarer Ausgabe] — WA Br. = Briefe
WCC	World Council of Churches

Introduction

1. The issue of papacy and church unity is among the thorniest ecumenical problems of the past and the present. It is also a topic that will be the most difficult to work out in Catholic-Lutheran relations. However, if the churches wish to make the biblical witness present and audible in all its unmistakably specific character to a world becoming more and more pluralistic, they will have to provide this witness and this ministry together and in communion with one another, simply for the sake of the credibility of the message. This communion of churches does not exist at the present time. To restore it belongs to the basic obligations of each Christian church. It is an obvious step, then, to examine the question: Can the Roman Catholic papacy be developed into an office that in fact serves *the communion of churches?*

2. After centuries of hard-fought controversies, Lutherans and Catholics are definitely not in agreement regarding the way in which papacy is exercised. Yet, they share a common concern about truth and ecclesial indefectibility that may turn out to be the common platform from which a future agreement about the Petrine ministry may develop. Recent developments in church and theology have witnessed a shift in attitude even here, at least among ecumenically aware theologians and church people on either side. The popes Paul VI and John Paul II were aware of the great ecumenical difficulties caused by the institution of papacy.[1] The prolific and courageous ecclesiological contribu-

---

1. See Thomas F. Stransky and John B. Sheerin, eds., *Doing the Truth in Charity: Statements of Pope Paul VI, Popes John Paul I, John Paul II, and the Secretariat for Promoting Christian Unity, 1964-1980* (New York: Paulist Press, 1982), p. 273.

tions of so many Catholic theologians, deeply committed to the ecumenical cause, have had a contagious effect. They have stimulated a daring project of rethinking positions that have been handed down but are now viewed by many as belonging to the past, and have created a climate of dialogue. Lutherans, for their part, can now feel more at ease when dealing with highly controversial or even explosive issues such as papacy and primacy. They can consider the possibility that the followers of the Reformation may have fallen victim to prejudices instead of reflecting the principles of the reformers themselves.

3. The recent change in attitude toward the possibility of a common understanding of papal ministry does in fact create a conciliatory atmosphere for the communication between the churches, but it still does not remove the factual historical development or invalidate and cancel the oppressive mortgage of history. Past history cannot be annulled, nor can it be revised; it remains as it is, and it is our task to arrive at an honest acknowledgment of what has actually happened. The negative legacy that we inherit and that weighs down on us was one of arrogantly casting blame on each other while seeking sole domination. But under favorable circumstances, history may be overcome, in the sense that Lutherans and Catholics might come to terms with their common past, including all their failures and shortcomings, even odium. From this common point of departure, then, the prospect opens up for a reasonable dialogue with the goal of church fellowship.[2]

4. The ecumenical challenge of those resolved to work toward a *common* future is to reshape declarations of intention into an effective reality in the life of the churches. On solemn occasions it is usually easy enough to surmount past tensions verbally; more often than not, however, this is just an aspiration without any ecumenical effect. Inner-church business goes on quietly as usual. Nobody should be blind to the fact that in many respects this is the actual ecumenical situation. To the extent, however, that this is the case, any ecumenical progress will be severely impeded. The churches are in need of a deep-reaching change of attitude toward one another. John Paul II would have la-

---

2. Heinrich Leipold sums up aptly the ecumenical advances since Vatican II in the area of papal ministry in his contribution, "Papsttum II," in *TRE* 25, p. 692 (1995), noting that the ecumenical dialogues since Vatican II have made several contributions to the theology of the papal office. They have "helped to clear up misunderstandings, in some areas to reconcile doctrinal positions formerly held to be incompatible, and in others to bring about convergences, so that a basic consensus has become apparent alongside a deep-rooted dissensus. Granting the range of disagreement that the dialogues have shown to persist, the decisive change for the churches of the Reformation in their experience with the papacy consists in this, that they perceive and recognize in it an office in the service of the Gospel."

beled it *conversion,* without which all interconfessional endeavors are in vain. Only too often they serve as ecumenical alibis at a time when one tries with considerable success to combine the official ecumenical commitment with a determined strengthening of traditional confessionalistic positions. Everyone committed to ecumenical dialogue should at least be attentive to this precarious situation.

5. Against the background of growing interest in the role of the papacy, the conferences as described in the Foreword,[3] and the subsequently founded *Gruppe von Farfa Sabina* have brought together ecumenical theologians for dialogue. This *Farfa Working Group on the Petrine Ministry* submits herewith its deliberations and reflections on the Petrine ministry in the context of a *communio ecclesiarum.*

6. In the course of these deliberations it became clearer that Lutherans and Catholics, despite many differences in the understanding of the papal office, have in common essential convictions and basic agreements, which may serve as starting points for a future accord:

- The church has the divine promise of abiding in the truth (cf. John 16:13; Matt. 16:18; 28:20; attested in numerous texts not only from the Catholic, but also the Lutheran tradition [e.g., Confessio Augustana, art. 7]).[4] Thus it is common Catholic and Lutheran conviction that the church as a fellowship of believers *(communio sanctorum)* shall in their totality be sustained in and never fall out of the truth *(sensus fidelium).* It may occasionally fall victim to all kinds of errors and defeats and even betray its Lord and Savior, but it will never cease to be the church. This fact of faith is expressed in the traditional concept of *indefectibilitas,* resp. *perennitas ecclesiae,* in the Lutheran context in the notion of *ecclesia mansura.*

- In conformity with this promise and corresponding to the trinitarian origin and nature of the church, but also for the sake of its witness and service, the communion of believers needs a visible and recognizable unity, and it is in need of concrete institutions to secure and maintain the unity of the church.

---

3. These conferences are documented in James F. Puglisi, ed., *How Can the Petrine Ministry Be a Service to the Unity of the Universal Church?* (Grand Rapids and Cambridge, UK: Eerdmans, 2010).

4. Agreement in this matter has been predominant in Catholic-Lutheran dialogues from the very beginning, e.g., Malta 22: ". . . Lutherans and Catholics are convinced that the Holy Spirit unceasingly leads and keeps the church in the truth. It is in this context that one must understand the concepts of indefectibility and infallibility . . ." *(GiA* [I], 173).

- Therefore the apostolic ministry is given by God as a "ministry of reconciliation" (2 Cor. 5:8-20) and thus as a specific tool to foster, strengthen, and serve the One Church by watchfully *(episkopeîn, episkopē)* taking care to hand on the authentic apostolic message and to preserve ecclesial unity.

7. Throughout history this ministry of *episkopē* has been exercised personally, collegially, and within the framework of synods and councils; as well as on different levels: locally, regionally, and universally.

8. On the level of the local church, government takes the form of the ministry of a pastor/parish priest who as a Christian is certainly "in" the community, but at the same time by virtue of the office is placed "over" it. This is repeated on the next level of government: the association of several local parishes (deanery, vicariate), which is led by a priest variously described as *dean, vicar, archpriest,* or *moderator.* Government is continued on the next or territorial level of the church: in a diocese, national church, or church province led by a bishop or other officeholder. It can happen that in the college of bishops of a country one bishop may be regarded as *primus inter pares* and described as *primate.*

9. On the universal level of the church this dimension of primacy is in no way alien to most confessions, even if the differences are here especially marked. Among Catholics, Orthodox, and Anglicans it is inseparably linked with the episcopal see of a particular city. It is most conspicuously present in the Roman Catholic Church with the Bishop of Rome as the bearer of the papal primacy of doctrine and jurisdiction. In the Orthodox churches of the East the Bishop of Constantinople is the Ecumenical Patriarch, while the Anglican churches have their primate in the Archbishop of Canterbury. In the Orthodox and Anglican churches a *preeminence of honor* and at least a *symbolic unifying role* is assigned to this office. The situation in most other churches (e.g., the Lutheran) is significantly different. A clear consciousness of their worldwide, universal community developed relatively late and led to the formation of confessional world families or world associations in the later nineteenth and especially the first half of the twentieth century. Though their structures are mainly of a communal, synodal, or conciliar type, they have not eschewed particular forms of leadership with a certain touch of primacy, for instance in the form of the offices of a President or a General Secretary.

10. Just as secular institutions are run by a responsible leadership, so it would be perfectly conceivable — with regard to the unity of the church in the *communio ecclesiarum* — to think of a totally pragmatic ministry of universal unity. However, such a pragmatic vision does not get to the heart of the matter,

because the primary theological controversy concerns the fundamental and constitutive necessity of a universal primacy for the very being of the church. On this point a common conviction seems, though, to be emerging:

(1) such a primacy is not necessary for salvation, and
(2) such a primacy is necessary only for the unity of the church and does not constitute her very being.

11. However, on this latter point no definite clarity has so far been achieved. Recent Roman Catholic statements (e.g., in the dialogue with the Anglican Communion) reveal important perspectives regarding the ministry of universal primacy as a constitutive part of the being of the church itself. Here clarification is still needed, before a Lutheran acceptance of *necessitas primatus universalis* is possible.[5] In the light of recent theological and ecumenical developments, however, such possible clarification does not seem a priori out of the question. If Christian unity is presently one of the primary "necessities of the Church," how then can papal primacy be designed in compliance with this *necessitas ecclesiae?*[6]

12. In spite of all improvements in the relationship between the confessions, however, the key question still arises if the papal ministry in general and the papal claim of universal primacy and infallibility particularly, as they have developed since the time of the Reformation, must still be seen as church divisive.

13. The efforts of the *Farfa Working Group on the Petrine Ministry* are to be understood as a modest response to the invitation extended by Pope John Paul II in his encyclical letter of May 25, 1995: *Ut unum sint.*[7] In it he proposed

5. See Chapter III.2.1.

6. This basic principle was also expressed by the Congregation for the Doctrine of Faith in this way: "The concrete contents of its exercise distinguish the Petrine ministry insofar as they faithfully express the application of its ultimate purpose (the unity of the Church) to the circumstances of time and place. The greater or lesser extent of these concrete contents will depend in every age on the *necessitas Ecclesiae.* The Holy Spirit helps the Church to recognize this *necessity,* and the Roman Pontiff, by listening to the Spirit's voice in the Churches, looks for the answer and offers it when and how he considers it appropriate" (from www.doctrina fidei.va/documents/rc_con_cfaith_doc_19981031_primato-successore-pietro_en.html#top). Same in *Il primato del successore di Pietro nel ministero della Chiesa: Considerazioni della Congregazione per la Dottrina della Fede, testo e commenti* (Vatican City: Libreria Editrice Vaticana, 2002), no. 12.

7. *Ut unum sint: Encyclical Letter of the Holy Father John Paul II on Commitment to Ecumenism* (London: Catholic Truth Society, 1995); also *AAS* 87 (1995): 921-82 or www.vatican

to "church leaders and . . . theologians" from churches, with whom the Roman Catholic Church finds itself in a "real but imperfect communion" . . . "to engage with [him] in a patient and fraternal dialogue" on the ministry of unity of the Bishop of Rome (UUS 88ff., especially 96), consciously intending to discard useless controversies and to overcome traditional prejudices, and seriously to consider how Christians in common could "find a way of exercising the primacy which, while in no way renouncing what is essential to its mission, is nonetheless open to a new situation" (UUS 95; cf. 89).

14. John Paul II was aware of the fact that the office of the Bishop of Rome as a visible sign and guarantor of ecclesial unity "constitutes a difficulty for most other Christians, whose memory is marked by certain painful recollections."[8] He left no doubt, however, as to the Catholic point of departure in this dialogue, though it itself constitutes the ecumenical problem:

> The Catholic Church, both in her *praxis* and in her solemn documents, holds that the communion of the particular Churches with the Church of Rome, and of their Bishops with the Bishop of Rome, is — in God's plan — an essential requisite of full and visible communion. Indeed full communion, of which the Eucharist is the highest sacramental manifestation, needs to be visibly expressed in a ministry in which all the Bishops recognize that they are united in Christ and all the faithful find confirmation for their faith. The first part of the Acts of the Apostles presents Peter as the one who speaks in the name of the apostolic group and who serves the unity of the community — all the while respecting the authority of James, the head of the Church in Jerusalem. This function of Peter must continue in the Church so that under her sole Head, who is Jesus Christ, she may be visibly present in the world as the communion of all his disciples.[9]

15. The Farfa Group decided, without however predetermining any theological details, to accept the invitation of the Pope and to put the issue on the agenda. This struck us as all the more obvious in that the ever-more painful lack of a universal ministry of unity over the course of Lutheran history had resulted in a certain provincialism and nationalism among Lutheran churches. In addition the realization grew that the Lutheran reformers had nothing in

---

.va/holy_father/john_paul_ii/encyclicals/documents/hf_jp-ii_enc_25051995_ut-unum-sint_en.html.

8. *UUS* 88; the Pope adds a request for forgiveness: "To the extent that we are responsible for these, I join my Predecessor Paul VI in asking forgiveness."

9. *UUS* 97.

principle against papacy, provided that it be subordinated to the primacy of the gospel and theologically interpreted and practically structured accordingly.[10] Furthermore, all historical uncertainties and theological difficulties concerning the origin and claim of papal authority notwithstanding, the central and guiding role of Rome and its bishop throughout Christian history seems to be a historical fact that is gaining ever more weight and ecumenical interest.[11]

16. In this light the Farfa Group raised the initial question: How could the papal ministry, as it has developed historically and as we know it today, become an instrument for the preservation of unity not only in the Roman Catholic Church, but also in the church universal (in terms of *communio ecclesiarum*), while remaining faithful to its own basic principles as they are primarily expressed in the dogmatic statements of the two Vatican Councils? The group thus made a clear distinction between papacy in its historical and present shape on the one hand and on the other the dogmatic content of the Petrine office as a service of unity for all churches.

17. This fundamental issue also determined the *modus procedendi* of the Farfa initiative. A group of Lutheran theologians and canonists took on the task, in collaboration with Catholic colleagues, of carefully investigating anew the basic historical documents that define the Roman Catholic view on papacy and its role in the life of the church(es). Such a close rereading of the key texts

10. This has been an issue for discussion ever since the beginning of the Catholic-Lutheran dialogue: ". . . in various dialogues, the *possibility* begins to emerge that the Petrine office of the Bishop of Rome also need not be excluded by Lutherans as a visible sign of the unity of the church as a whole, 'insofar as [this office] is subordinated to the primacy of the gospel by theological reinterpretation and practical restructuring.'" *The Ministry of the Church* [1981], 73, in *GiA* (I), 271; cf. Malta Report [1972], 66, in *GiA* (I), 184. See also Walter Kasper, *Harvesting the Fruits: Aspects of Christian Faith in Ecumenical Dialogue* (London and New York: Continuum, 2009), pp. 48-158.

11. "Es ist ein Faktum der Geschichte des Christentums, daß seit dem Ende der Jerusalemer Urgemeinde Rom das historische Zentrum der Christenheit geworden ist. Wenn irgendein christlicher Bischof in Situationen, in denen das erforderlich sein sollte, für die ganze Christenheit sprechen kann, dann wird das wohl am ehesten der Bischof von Rom sein. Trotz aller bitteren Auseinandersetzungen infolge des chronischen machtpolitischen Mißbrauchs der Autorität Roms gibt es hier keine realistische Alternative. Das ist heute sowohl der Weltöffentlichkeit als auch den meisten Kirchen der Christenheit bewußt. Die Tatsache dieses Vorrangs der römischen Gemeinde und ihres Bischofs in der Christenheit sollte unbefangen anerkannt werden." Wolfhart Pannenberg, *Systematische Theologie,* vol. 3 (Göttingen: Vandenhoeck & Ruprecht, 1993), p. 458. See also *Kirche und Kirchengemeinschaft: Bericht der Internationalen Römisch-Katholisch–Altkatholischen Dialogkommission* (Paderborn: Bonifatius; Frankfurt am Main: Verlag Otto Lembeck, 2009), pp. 19-28.

of Vatican I and II in common and in the light of recent Catholic theology, with the aim of removing what continues to prohibit Catholics and Lutherans from agreement in this area, has opened up new avenues for a differentiated understanding and reassessment of papal primacy. This in turn allowed for a fresh view of infallibility and universal jurisdiction, which could serve as the theological basis for a possible rapprochement between the two churches and a future Lutheran recognition of the Petrine function as a ministry of unity in the service of the *communio ecclesiarum.*

Luther's Critique of Pope and Papacy and the Roman Reaction

18. The Lutheran Reformation did not begin with a rejection of the papal ministry. Even though Luther's theses on indulgences of 1517 refer again and again to the limits of the pope's spiritual authority, they do not question the papal ministry as such, and the same remained true for almost the next two years. In the midst of the whole conflict with Rome, one comes across statements by Luther that forcefully speak in favor of the pope, of the papal ministry, and of papal authority. In his early manhood he had "honestly thought no differently about the pope, councils and universities than was commonly done," said Luther in 1521 in his pamphlet against Jakob Latomus, who had reproached his deferential attitude to the pope as hypocrisy.[1] Luther did not see any contradiction between the firm insistence on his Reformation convictions, on the one hand, and his assent to the papal ministry, on the other. And so he refused to see here the unpardonable contradiction that his opponents charged him with and that would very soon become for them the crucial point of their critique. The questioning and the rejection of the papal ministry only hesitatingly gained hold of Luther. They very soon became linked, even if at first only allusively and in hypothetical terms, with the notion of "the Antichrist." Not until the months between June and October 1520 did they achieve full expression. Thereafter everything Luther says about the pope and the papal ministry seems to be predicated on the "Antichrist" polemic, which runs through his polemical writings to the end of his life.

---

1. Weimar Edition of Luther's Works (= *WA*) 8, 20-22, 45.

19. Luther was forced by the controversy with his opponents to consider the issue of papacy. The conflict over material dogmatic questions, as e.g., the right understanding of indulgences, developed into a dispute about authorities.

A. Holy Scripture, Tradition, and Teaching Office

1. Luther's Appeal to Holy Scripture and His Critique of the Teaching Office

20. On 31 October 1517 Martin Luther invited friends and colleagues to Wittenberg to take part in a disputation on indulgences and to this end drew up ninety-five theses, which he also sent to Albrecht of Brandenburg, Archbishop of Magdeburg and Halberstadt, and concurrently, since 1514, Archbishop of Mainz. Due to the notorious course of events leading up to his appointment to head this additional archdiocese, Albrecht of Brandenburg had been the real trigger of the conflict over indulgences.[2] A first semi-official reaction to Luther's theses was not slow in coming. It came from the Italian papal court theologian Sylvester Prierias OP (alias Silvestro Mazzolini) in his all too hastily written treatise *Dialogus de potestate Papae in Lutheri Conclusiones*[3] in 1518. The introductory part[4] of this Dialogue is quite remarkable. Prierias enunciates in it four fundamental principles, which would then mark the future lines of conflict:

- the pope is the head of all churches;
- the pope could not err in questions of faith and morals;
- only through the power of the pope did Holy Scripture have strength and validity in the church;
- whoever says the church cannot do what in fact she does should be considered a heretic.

2. Bernhard Lohse, "Albrecht von Brandenburg und Luther," in *Erzbischof Albrecht von Brandenburg (1490-1545): Ein Kirchen- und Reichsfürst der Frühen Neuzeit*, ed. Friedhelm Jürgensmeier (Frankfurt am Main: Verlag Josef Knecht, 1991), pp. 73-83.

3. In: Erlanger Ausgabe: *D. Martini Lutheri opera latina varii argumenti ad reformationis historiam imprimis pertinentia*, vol. 1 (Frankfurt am Main: C. Heyder; Erlangen: H. Zimmer, 1865), pp. 344ff.

4. Also in *Quellen zur Geschichte des Papsttums und des römischen Katholizismus*, 1st-5th ed., ed. Carl Mirbt, 6th ed., ed. Kurt Aland, vol. 1: *Von den Anfängen bis zum Tridentinum* (Tübingen: J. C. B. Mohr [Paul Siebeck], 1967), pp. 501-3, no. 787.

21. Luther replied to this "Dialogue" with a no less hastily written answer.[5] He countered the "fundamental principles" of Prierias, which he simply ignored, with three very skillfully chosen "foundations" of his own:

- first, he responded with two references to Holy Scripture: namely, 1 Thessalonians 5:21 ("Test everything; hold fast what is good") and Galatians 1:8 ("Even if . . . an angel from heaven should preach to you a gospel contrary to that which we preached to you, let him be accursed." Thus, Luther, citing biblical quotations, referred to the gospel as the only norm for the doctrine and action of the church.
- second, Luther referred to Augustine, who holds only the books of the Bible free from error.
- third, Luther referred to canon law, which does not permit anything to be presented to the people that is not contained in Holy Scripture.[6]

22. The fundamental principles of Prierias are, according to Luther's express statement, without any foundation in Holy Scripture, in the Church Fathers, and in canon law.[7] What is more, Luther argued there are no rational grounds for them. Luther knew himself to be in agreement with the most important church authorities that had professed Holy Scripture as the norm of church doctrine and action.[8] The whole conflict between Luther and the

5. *Ad Dialogum Silvestri Prieriatis de potestate papae responsio* (1518), in *WA* 1, 644-86.

6. Cf. Martin Brecht, *Martin Luther: Sein Weg zur Reformation, 1483-1521* (Stuttgart: Calwer Verlag, 1981), pp. 235-36.

7. "sine scriptura, sine patribus, sine canonibus, denique sine ullis rationibus" (*WA* 1, 647, 32-33).

8. Already Thomas Aquinas had, with reference to Augustine, taught the principle of "Scripture alone," for according to him what is binding for the faith is fully and expressly contained in Scripture ("Innititur enim fides nostra revelationi Apostolis et Prophetis factae, qui canonicos libros scripserunt: non autem revelationi, si qua fuit aliis doctoribus facta," *Sth* I 1,8 ad 2; Bruno Decker, "Sola Scriptura bei Thomas von Aquin," in *Universitas: Dienst an Wahrheit und Leben. FS Bischof Albert Stohr*, 2 vols., ed. Ludwig Lenhart (Mainz: Matthias Grünewald, 1960), vol. 1, pp. 117-29; Bruno Decker, "Schriftprinzip und Ergänzungstradition in der Lehre des hl. Thomas von Aquin," in *Schrift und Tradition*, ed. Deutsche Arbeitsgemeinschaft für Mariologie, Hermann Josef Brosch (Essen: Driewer, 1962), pp. 191-221; Yves Congar, "'Traditio' und 'sacra doctrina' bei Thomas von Aquin," in *Kirche und Überlieferung*, ed. Johannes Betz and Heinrich Fries (Freiburg, Basel, Vienna: Herder, 1960), pp. 170-210; Otto Hermann Pesch, *Theologie der Rechtfertigung bei Martin Luther und Thomas von Aquin* (Mainz: Matthias Grünewald, 1967), pp. 728 and 877f.; Otto Hermann Pesch, *Das Zweite Vatikanische Konzil (1962-1965): Vorgeschichte — Verlauf — Ergebnisse — Nachgeschichte*, 2nd ed. (Würzburg: Echter Verlag, 1994), p. 280.

papalist-Roman party in the sixteenth century (other parties, such as the con-ciliar party, did indeed exist at the time) is already, in some sense, contained *in nuce* in the dispute between Prierias and Luther in 1518. This dispute re-volved around fundamental questions that, in the further course of the Refor-mation, would be expressed in the following questions:

- What is the material norm that determines what should hold good in the church: the word of Holy Scripture (according to Luther) or the word of the church authority, and in particular of the pope (according to Prierias and, in the further course of the conflict, the theologians of the papal party)?
- Is Holy Scripture as the Word of God to be accepted as a fundamental criterion of the word of the church as a human word?
- Where can the truth that is needed for salvation be found: in the apostolic transmission of Holy Scripture or also in the post-apostolic doctrinal and liturgical tradition of the church?
- How is a faithful interpretation of Holy Scripture to be achieved? Is this only the prerogative of the papal teaching office, or are others in a position to interpret it? Is Holy Scripture clear and intelligible, or does it need the papal teaching office to clarify obscure passages in it?

23. These questions imposed themselves in this conflict of views not least because the affirmations of Prierias were understood as the official position of Rome. Yet this was far from being self-evident, since canon law was also open to other interpretations. In the bitter disputes of that time the possibility of a fundamental theological dialogue was not taken into consideration.

24. In his approach Luther showed himself to be no biblical fundamen-talist who could rest his case on isolated individual biblical passages. In his treatise *Von Menschenlehre zu meiden* (Of human doctrine and how to avoid it) of 1522 he expressly states, without any possibility of doubt, that the whole of Holy Scripture was directed at Christ alone.[9] In his later text of 1525, *De servo arbitrio,* he replied to Erasmus by posing a question: "Tolle Christum e scripturis, quid amplius in illis invenies?"[10] Christ is the Word of God who became flesh; and since Scripture has only this single content, Jesus Christ, it is *ipso facto* the Word of God. No less clear is Luther in his foreword to his

9. *WA* 10/II, (61-71) 72-92, here 73, 15f.

10. *WA* 18, (551-99) 600-787, here 606, 29 ("If you take Christ out of Scripture, what else will you find in it?").

Sermons on the First Epistle of Peter of 1523: everything that the Apostle wrote is, he claimed, one single gospel:

> The word "Gospel" signifies nothing else than a sermon or report concerning the grace and mercy of God merited and acquired through the Lord Jesus Christ with his Death. Actually, the Gospel is not what one finds in books and what is written in letters of the alphabet: it is rather an oral sermon and a living Word, a voice that resounds throughout the world and is proclaimed publicly, so that one hears it everywhere.[11]

25. Already in 1522 Luther had, in his *Kirchenpostille*, in a spiritual and theological reflection on the meaning of Matthew 2:1-12, fundamentally formulated why a New Testament was necessary:

> It would not at all be in keeping with the way of the New Testament to write books on Christian doctrine. It was not books, but apostles that were needed. In all places there should be fine, godly, learned, spiritual, diligent preachers without books, who extract the living word from all Scripture and unceasingly inculcate it into the people, just as the apostles did. For before they wrote, they first of all preached to the people by word of mouth and converted them, and this was their real apostolic and New Testament work. However, the need to write books was a serious decline and a lack of the Spirit which necessity forced on us; it is not the manner of the New Testament. For when heretics, false teachers, and all manner of errors arose in the place of pious preachers giving the flock of Christ poison as pasture, then every last thing that could and needed to be done had to be attempted, so that at least some sheep might be saved from the wolves. So they began to write in order to lead the flock of Christ as much as possible by Scripture into Scripture. They wanted to ensure that the sheep could feed themselves and hence protect themselves against the wolves, if their shepherds failed to feed them or were in danger of becoming wolves too.[12]

26. That the church had produced the biblical canon does not mean, Luther taught, that she was therefore mistress over Scripture; on the contrary she is

---

11. *WA* 12, 259-399, here 259, 7-13; *Luther's Works*, vol. 30: *The Catholic Epistles*, ed. Jaroslav Pelikan and Walter A. Hansen (Saint Louis: Concordia, 1967), p. 3.

12. *WA* 10/1,1, 626,15–627,10; *Luther's Works*, vol. 52: *Sermons II*, ed. Hans J. Hillerbrand (Philadelphia: Fortress Press, 1974), p. 206 (here summary of Luther's text).

subject to the Word of God. For she testifies, that she is a "subordinate" of it and confesses that the church is confirmed by her "judge and sovereign," the gospel and Holy Scripture.[13] If we consider the content of these Luther texts as a whole, it is understandable why, according to Luther, Scripture is "imposed" in the power of the Holy Spirit as witness of the Word of God that became flesh in Jesus Christ. He is its center and determines its content. Although Holy Scripture was written by men, its real author is the Holy Spirit. Scripture, however, can only be interpreted in the Spirit in which it was written; with this Spirit the baptized have been imbued in baptism, so that everyone in the church may grasp this single content of Scripture if they read it in the Spirit in which it was written; the content of Scripture will then be revealed in all its clarity and transparency. So, for Martin Luther, self-interpretation of Holy Scripture and interpretation in and through the Holy Spirit belong together.[14]

The consequences of this theological position are no less clear. Holy Scripture alone is the sole norm for church doctrine, worship and the Sacraments, church action, ministers in the church, and so on; as its "subordinate" it is the church's job to "preach" the salvation obtained once and for all and for everyone by Christ's death and resurrection; the preaching of the Word of God establishes faith in which alone the believer is enabled to share in the salvation won by Christ. The church cannot make such sharing in salvation dependent on any conditions set by the church; the granting of salvation is and remains unconditional.[15] Everything that has currency in the church must be based on Scripture. Church doctrine, worship and sacraments, church action, church ministers etc. are to be reformed, or even abolished, if they cannot fundamentally be reconciled with the content of Holy Scripture, or directly contradict it (e.g. the late medieval theories of the mass); they are also to be altered if they obscure the witness of Scripture, obstruct our devotion to Jesus Christ or even divert us from him. The Christian system that reigned in Luther's time was placed in question by his writings. Scripture, tradition, teaching authority of the church or the pope,

13. See Luther's *Artikel wider die ganze Satansschule und alle Pforten der Hölle*, 1530 (*WA* 30/II, [413-19], 420-27, here 420 and 424).

14. See Luther's *Assertio omnium articulorum M. Lutheri per bullam Leonis X. novissimam damnatorum*, 1520 (*WA* 7, 94-151, here 7, 96-97).

15. In the semi-official document of the Joint Roman Catholic-Lutheran Commission, in the "Malta Report" of 1972 (*GiA* [I], 174-75), and in "Church and Justification" of 1993 (*GiA* II, 488-89 and 525-26) this point of view is underlined in common: ". . . all traditions and institutions of the church are subject to the criterion which asks whether they are enablers of the proper proclamation of the gospel and do not obscure the unconditional character of the gift of salvation" (*GiA* [I], 175).

and their relation to each other, became the bones of contention that still stand at the centre of the debate, also in the context of our present discussion.

2. The Roman Reaction in the Sixteenth and in the Following Centuries

27. So how did the Roman Catholic Church react after the excommunication of the reformers? The answer to this question can be deduced, on the one hand, from the decisions of the Council of Trent and, on the other, from the history of post-tridentine theology and church. The Council of Trent during its fourth session on April 8, 1546 issued the following decree:

> . . . that in the Church errors be removed and the purity of the Gospel be preserved. This Gospel was promised of old through the prophets in the Sacred Scriptures; Our Lord Jesus Christ, Son of God, first promulgated it from his own lips; he in turn ordered that it be preached through the apostles to all creatures as the source of all saving truth and norms of conduct. The Council clearly perceives that this truth and rule are contained in the written books and unwritten traditions which have come down to us, having been received by the apostles from the mouth of Christ himself or from the apostles by the dictation of the Holy Spirit, and have been transmitted as it were from hand to hand *(per manus traditae)*. Following, then, the example of the orthodox Fathers, it receives and venerates with the same sense of loyalty and reverence all the books of the Old and New Testament — for the one God is the author of both — together with all the traditions concerning faith and practice, as coming from the mouth of Christ or being inspired by the Holy Spirit and preserved in continuous succession in the Catholic Church.[16]

28. The draft of this decree prepared for the Council of Trent, affirming that saving truth had been preserved partly in Scripture, partly in unwritten traditions, was at the last moment not adopted by the Council. Instead of this formulation, it was simply stated that saving truth is contained in Scripture (in libris scriptis) and in unwritten traditions (sine scripto traditionibus). According to the groundbreaking studies of Joseph Rupert Geiselmann,[17] the Council of Trent understood the unwritten traditions to mean the following:

---

16. *DH* 1501; *ND* 210.

17. Josef Rupert Geiselmann, "Das Konzil von Trient über das Verhältnis der Heiligen

> Apostolic traditions are the traditions within the Church that were originally transmitted to the Church not through Scriptures, but through (the living word of) the apostles and that have come down to us through the unbroken apostolic succession of bishops in their proclamation of the Word of God . . . , insofar as they have their origin in Christ or in the Holy Spirit . . . and have as their object faith and morals.[18]

29. By replacing the "partly — partly" formulation in the original draft by "and," the Council of Trent, according to Geiselmann, had evaded making a decision about the relation of the written apostolic tradition (Holy Scripture) to the unwritten apostolic (ecclesial) tradition (*successio apostolica* through the bishops).[19] In contrast to the Reformation position, in which the sufficiency of Holy Scripture is unambiguously taught, the Council of Trent neither affirmed "the sufficiency of the content of Holy Scripture . . . nor . . . determined the relation of Scripture and Tradition in the sense of 'partly-partly.' "[20]

30. The whole of post-tridentine Roman Catholic theology, by reverting to pre-tridentine controversial theologians, however, came to understand the decision of the Council of Trent as if Trent had definitively decided that the saving truth was preserved *partly* in Scripture and *partly* in the *sine scripto traditionibus.* So the *Catechismus Romanus,* written on commission from the Council of Trent and published under Pius V in 1566, formulated the relation between Scripture and Tradition as follows:

> Omnis autem doctrinae ratio, quae fidelibus tradenda sit, verbo dei continetur, quod in Scripturam Traditionesque distributum est.[21]

Schrift und der nicht geschriebenen Traditionen: Sein Missverständnis in der nachtridentinischen Theologie und die Überwindung dieses Missverständnisses," in Heinrich Bacht, Heinrich Fries, and Josef Rupert Geiselmann, *Die mündliche Überlieferung: Beiträge zum Begriff der Tradition,* ed. Michael Schmaus (Munich: Max Hueber Verlag, 1957), pp. 123-206; — Josef Rupert Geiselmann, "Schrift — Tradition — Kirche: Ein ökumenisches Problem," in *Begegnung der Christen: Studien evangelischer und katholischer Theologen,* ed. Maximilian Roesle and Oscar Cullmann (Stuttgart: Evangelisches Verlagswerk, Frankfurt am Main: Verlag Josef Knecht, 1959), pp. 131-59.

18. Geiselmann, "Das Konzil von Trient" (see note 17), p. 136f.

19. Geiselmann, "Schrift — Tradition — Kirche" (see note 17), p. 142.

20. Geiselmann, "Schrift — Tradition — Kirche" (see note 17), p. 141.

21. *Catechismus Romanus: Prooemium, Questio XII,* ed. Adolf Buse, 3rd ed. (Bielefeld, Leipzig: Verlag von Velhagen und Klasing, 1867), p. 8: "The content of all teaching that is to be

31. Already Johann Eck in his treatise on the Mass *De sacrificio missae libri tres* (1526) had cited the *De ecclesiastica hierarchia* written by Pseudo-Dionysius Areopagita in its Latin translation by Ambrosius Traversari Camaldulensis and there found the formula *partim scriptis, partim non scriptis constitutionibus*[22] and drew the following conclusion from it: ". . . apostoli partim scriptis, partim non scriptis institutionibus mysteria nobis tradiderunt."[23] This *partly — partly* formulation is already found expressed in pre-tridentine controversial theology,[24] but — as explained above — in the last moment was not adopted by the Council of Trent. Immediately after the Council, however, it was understood and disseminated in the sense of pre-tridentine controversial theology, both in the Catechismus Romanus and especially through Petrus Canisius and Robert Bellarmine, the foremost exponents of the Counter-Reformation.[25] It then became the standard formula of Roman Catholic controversial theology in the following centuries. This formula was subjected to several modifications in the periods of the Enlightenment, classicism, and romanticism; alongside a *sive — sive* formula, it was altered into a *totaliter in traditione, partim in scriptura*. A quite different concept was not developed until late by Johann Evangelist Kuhn (1806-1887), after he had long espoused the *partim — partim* formula: he then reformulated it as *totum in scriptura* and *totum in traditione*.[26] This formula, however, was not accepted among Catholics in the mid-nineteenth century. Through the dominating neo-scholasticism the *partim — partim* formula led in the nineteenth century to

---

imparted to the faithful is contained in the Word of God, which is distributed in Scripture and the Traditions."

22. See Johannes Eck, *De sacrificio missae libri tres (1526)*, ed. Erwin Iserloh, Vinzenz Pfnür, and Peter Fabisch (Münster: Aschendorffsche Verlagsbuchhandlung, 1982), pp. 81-83, here 82 (Liber secundus, Cap. I); on the interpretation see Josef Rupert Geiselmann, "Das Konzil von Trient" (see note 17), pp. 140-47.

23. Johannes Eck, *De sacrificio missae libri tres*, p. 83.

24. See the instances cited in Geiselmann, "Das Konzil von Trient" (see note 17), pp. 138-63.

25. For an exhaustive treatment see Geiselmann, "Das Konzil von Trient" (see note 17), pp. 168-77.

26. Geiselmann, "Das Konzil von Trient" (see note 17), pp. 200-206. According to Geiselmann, Kuhn's solution would have meant "pulling post-tridentine controversial theology up by the roots" (p. 200), Scripture transmitting the gospel as truth of Revelation, while the tradition that has become translated into writing of the truth of Revelation transmits the gospel in the form of its interpretation and its authoritative understanding. According to Edmund Schlink this means real progress for the ecumenical debate though he points to the danger of a traditionalist positivism that is implicit in this formula: Edmund Schlink, *Ökumenische Dogmatik: Grundzüge* (Göttingen: Vandenhoeck & Ruprecht, 1983), pp. 690f.

the theory of the twin sources of divine revelation. This theory was further developed in the First Vatican Council and was firmly maintained as the church's doctrine right down to the Second Vatican Council. This explains the doggedness with which the curial party at Vatican Council II fought for the maintenance of this concept as handed down by tradition.

32. With the aid of the two-source theory of revelation, one can understand better the two Marian dogmas: the dogma of the Immaculate Conception of Mary (1854) and the dogma of the Assumption of Mary (1950). It is implied in the formulation that the church is "the watchful guardian and defender of the dogmas deposited with her" (DH 2802). The Bulla *Ineffabilis Deus* of 1854, which dogmatized the doctrine of the Immaculate Conception, states that the church only makes clear what "the faith of the Fathers has transmitted," with nothing changed or added (DH 2802). On the other hand, it is not claimed that this doctrine can be found in Holy Scripture.[27] Therefore, nothing hinders, according to Pius IX, the infallible definition of the *Immaculata Conceptio* of Mary as divinely revealed truth, "by the authority of our Lord Jesus Christ, of the blessed apostles Peter and Paul, and our own authority":

> [W]e declare, pronounce and define: the doctrine which holds that the most Blessed Virgin Mary was, from the first moment of her conception, by a singular grace and privilege of almighty God and in view of the merits of Christ Jesus the Saviour of the human race, preserved immune from all stain of original sin, is revealed by God, and, therefore, firmly and constantly to be believed by all the faithful.[28]

27. "Christi enim ecclesia, sedula depositorum apud se dogmatum custos et vindex, nihil in his umquam permutat, nihil minuit, nihil addit, sed omni industria vetera fideliter sapienterque tractando si qua antiquitus informata sunt et Patrum fides sevit, ita limare, expolire studet, ut prisca illa caelestis doctrinae dogmata accipiunt evidentiam, lucem, distinctionem, sed retineant plenitudinem, integritatem, proprietatem, ac in suo tantum genere crescant, in eodem scilicet dogmate, eodem sensu eademque sententia" (*DH* 2802). ET: "For the Church of Christ, watchful guardian that she is, and defender of the dogmas deposited with her, never changes anything, never diminishes anything, never adds anything to them; but with all diligence she treats the ancient documents faithfully and wisely; if they really are of ancient origin and if the faith of the Fathers has transmitted them, she strives to investigate and explain them in such a way that the ancient dogmas of heavenly doctrine will be made evident and clear, but will retain their full, integral, and proper nature, and will grow only within their own genus — that is, within the same dogma, in the same sense and the same meaning."

28. ". . . declaramus, pronuntiamus et definimus, doctrinam, quae tenet, beatissimam Virginem Mariam in primo instanti suae conceptionis fuisse singulari omnipotentis Dei gratia et privilegio, intuitu meritorum Christi Iesu Salvatoris humani generis, ab omni originalis culpae

33. The Apostolic Constitution *Munificentissimus Deus* of 1950 reflects with regard to the Holy Scripture the relationship between Jesus and Mary, saying:

> All these proofs and considerations of the holy Fathers and the theologians are based upon the Sacred Writings as their ultimate foundation. These set the loving Mother of God as it were before our very eyes as most intimately joined to her divine Son and as always sharing his lot. Consequently it seems impossible to think of her, the one who conceived Christ, brought him forth, nursed him with her milk, held him in her arms, and clasped him to her breast, as being apart from him in body, even though not in soul, after this earthly life. Since our Redeemer is the Son of Mary, he could not do otherwise, as the perfect observer of God's law, than to honor, not only his eternal Father, but also his most beloved Mother. And, since it was within his power to grant her this great honor, to preserve her from the corruption of the tomb, we must believe that he really acted in this way.[29]

34. According to *Munificentissimus Deus* the typology of Eve and Mary of the Fathers of the Ancient Church is much more important for the dogma of the Assumption of Mary than the preceding, rather vague, biblical speculations:

> We must remember especially that . . . the Virgin Mary has been designated by the holy Fathers as the new Eve, who, although subject to the new Adam, is most intimately associated with him. . . .[30]

---

labe praeservatam immunem, esse a Deo revelatam atque idcirco ab omnibus fidelibus firmiter constanterque credendam" (*DH* 2803; *ND* 709).

29. "Haec omnia Sanctorum Patrum ac theologorum argumenta considerationesque Sacris Litteris tamquam ultimo fundamento nituntur; quae quidem almam Dei Matrem nobis veluti ante oculos proponunt divino Filio suo coniunctissimam, eiusque semper participantem sortem. Quamobrem quasi impossibile videtur eam cernere, quae Christum concepit, peperit, suo lacte aluit, eumque inter ulnas habuit pectorique obstrinxit suo, ab eodem post terrestrem hanc vitam, etsi non anima, corpore tamen separatam. [Redemptor noster] haud poterat profecto . . . praeter Aeternum Patrem, Matrem quoque suam dilectissimam non honorare. Atqui, cum eam posset tam magno honore exornare, ut eam a sepulcri corruptione servaret incolumem, id reapse fecisse credendum est" (*DH* 3900; *Munificentissimus Deus,* no. 38).

30. "Maxime autem illud memorandum est. . . . Mariam Virginem a Sanctis Patribus veluti novam Hevam proponi novo Adae, etsi subiectam, arctissime coniunctam . . ." (*DH* 3901; *Munificentissimus Deus,* no. 39).

35. The result of consulting the Holy Scripture and the tradition of the church is the dogmatization of the doctrine of the Assumption of Mary:

> [B]y the authority of our Lord Jesus Christ, of the Blessed Apostles Peter and Paul, and by our own authority, we pronounce, declare, and define it to be a divinely revealed dogma: that the Immaculate Mother of God, the ever Virgin Mary, having completed the course of her earthly life, was assumed body and soul into heavenly glory.[31]

36. The dogmas of 1854 and of 1950 reveal the theological problems of the — formal — theory of the twin sources of divine revelation. This theory has immediate consequences for the contents of the doctrines of faith. It contains within itself and as such, as well as in its implications, weighty complications for the ecumenical dialogue. To be sure, this form of Roman Catholic mariology represents an ecumenical challenge. But a response to this challenge cannot possibly be given apart from reconsidering the theological presuppositions. Neither can an ecumenical debate on Mary be conducted in isolation from such reconsideration. The problems created by the two-source theory of divine revelation can only be solved if one agrees with Thomas Aquinas[32] and Martin Luther that binding subjects of faith have to be based explicitly on Holy Scripture. This alone enables a new and better understanding of the biblical message and a fruitful ecumenical dialogue about Mary.

B. The Papacy

1. The Multilayered Judgment on Papal Ministry in the Lutheran Reformation

37. In Luther's writings we find repeated statements that break through the purely polemical treatment of the papal question and speak of the papal office as a *possibility* in the church. Especially interesting is what he wrote in 1533, looking back on the Imperial Diet in Augsburg. Though he had then criticized

---

31. ". . . auctoritate Domini Nostri Iesu Christi, Beatorum Apostolorum Petri et Pauli ac Nostra pronuntiamus, declaramus et definimus divinitus revelatum dogma esse: Immaculatam Deiparam semper Virginem Mariam, expleto terrestris vitae cursu, fuisse corpore et anima ad caelestem gloriam assumptam" (*DH* 3903; *Munificentissimus Deus,* no. 44; official translation, cf. *ND* 715).

32. *STh* I, 1,8 ad 2; see note 8 above.

the *Confessio Augustana* in particular for having passed over in silence "the question of the pope as Antichrist,"[33] and was ready to fill this gap with a document on the idolization of the pope,[34] Luther said three years later:

> Wir haben uns bis da her (d.h. bis jetzt) allezeit, und sonderlich auff dem Reichstage zu Augspurg, gar demütiglich erboten, dem Bapst und Bisschoven, das wir nicht wolten ir Kirchen rechte und gewalt zu reissen, sondern, wo sie uns nicht zu unchristlichen Artikeln zwüngen, gern von ihnen geweihet und regirt sein. . . . [We have until now at all times, and especially at the Imperial Diet in Augsburg, quite humbly offered to the pope and bishops not to strip their church of rights and power, but would be glad, on the contrary, to be ordained and governed by them, so long as they did not force un-Christian articles on us. . . .][35]

38. Some time later, in October 1535, Luther wrote in a letter to the preachers in Soest:

> [I]ch will noch sagen und zugeben will der Papst das Evangelion frei und rein lassen gehen, wie er schuldig ist zu tun, so will ich meiner Person ihn lassen sein, was er selber will. . . . [I wish further to say and to concede, that if the pope is willing to leave the gospel free and pure, as is his duty to do, I would be willing to submit my person to him. . . .][36]

39. Best known and most striking of all are no doubt Luther's statements in his Commentary on Galatians of 1531/1535, in which he once again makes it known that he would "gladly submit to the rule of the pope" ["dominium Papae libenter ferremus"], and that he would "honor him and respect his person, if he [the pope] would only be willing to leave my conscience free, and not compel me to slander God himself" [. . . Papam quoque venerabor et colam personatum ipsius, modo conscientiam mihi liberam relinquat nec cogat me ipsum Deum laedere"].[37]

40. "What we desire is that God's glory and the righteousness of the faith be preserved intact, so that we ourselves may be saved." Luther then continues with the often-cited sentence:

33. *WA Br* 5, 496, 9: ". . . maxime de antichristo Papa. . . ."
34. Cf. *WA* 30/II, 471.
35. *WA* 38, 195, 17-21.
36. *WA* 38, 397, 12-14.
37. *WA* 40/I, 177, 26-27, and 22-23.

> Once we obtain [what we ask, namely] the acknowledgment that God alone justifies from pure grace through Christ, then we are willing not only to carry the pope in our hands, but also to kiss his feet.[38]

41. Undoubtedly these and similar statements in Luther's writings have a quite clearly *conditional* character, that is, they make the possibility of an assent to the papal ministry depend on conditions that all ultimately lead to the demand that it be liberated from its "antichristian" features and — summa summarum — "permit the Gospel." Though Luther doubted that such a renewed papal ministry would or could ever be achieved, these statements show a *basic willingness* to accept it. So in Luther we encounter — albeit with very different emphases — two attitudes to the papal ministry: on the one hand, the radical repudiation of and, on the other, a conditional assent to the papal ministry as a possible theme of Luther's theology. That is the objective, and apparently contradictory, state of the case that can be deduced from Luther's writings.

42. If this objective fact is not to be distorted just to his polemical side, the question is posed: How does Luther's admittedly occasional, and yet repeatedly expressed openness to a renewed papal ministry relate to the whole breadth of his radical papal critique?

43. Discounting attempts to explain it in contextual or psychological terms, the only plausible explanation of this apparently contradictory fact lies in the *nature of Luther's papal critique,* which remains constant in him from the very beginning. It is precisely the polemically unparalleled "Antichrist" verdict that shows this. It is not a sweeping and undifferentiated judgment on the papal ministry as such. Rather, the "Antichrist" verdict represents in Luther's polemic the biblical abbreviation for equally fundamental and precise theological accusations that Luther raised against the papacy of his time. If one leaves out of account such accusations as lack of written foundation for the papal ministry,

38. "Sed hoc quaerimus, ut stet gloria Dei et iustitia fidei illaesa conservetur, ut simus nos salvi et ipsi. Hoc impetrato, scilicet quod solus Deus ex mera gratia per Christum iustificet, non solum volumus Papam in manibus portare, imo etiam ei osculari pedes" (*WA* 40/I, 181, 10-13). Luther repeats this assertion in almost identical words later: "Pope, I want to kiss your feet and recognize you as supreme bishop, once you will have prayed to my Christ and permitted us to have forgiveness of sins and eternal life through his death and Resurrection, and not through the observation of your traditions" ["Papa, ego volo tibi osculari pedes teque agnoscere summum pontificem, si adoraveris Christum meum et permiseris, quod per ipsius mortem et resurrectionem habeamus remissionem peccatorum et vitam aeternam, non per observationem tuarum traditionum"] (357, 18-21).

claims to worldly power and the lack of a secular or ecclesial mandate,[39] accusations that Luther did admittedly and forcefully make, but that do not constitute the decisive "antichristian" factors, it is in the last analysis three closely connected features that distinguish the pope as "Antichrist" in Luther's view:

- Just as an essential feature of the "Antichrist" is "soli sibi ius interpretandae scripturae arrogabit" ["to claim for himself alone the right to interpret the Scripture"],[40] so the pope too "interprets the Scripture exclusively according to his own understanding" and does not wish to let himself be ruled by it.[41]
- The papacy has added new dogma and demands to the Word of God — and to the laws based on this Word — and equates them with the words and commandments of God.[42]
- The pope "will not permit Christians to be saved without his power" and without them being "obedient to him." [Der Papst will "die Christen nicht selig werden lassen ohn sein Gewalt" und ohne dass sie "ihm gehorsam" sind.][43]

44. These three accusations form the theological core of the biblical and mythological "Antichrist" verdict. Taken together, they point to features of the papal ministry that do not apply irremediably and for all time to the papal ministry *as such,* but represent *deformations* of it and its exercise. The papacy had been free of such deformities, said Luther, until the time of Gregory I, the "last bishop of Rome."[44] It could be freed of them once again.

45. Those statements of Luther that express a conditional assent to the papal ministry refer precisely to these historical deformations. So these statements *qualify* Luther's papal critique in a decisive way. They show that Luther's papal critique, even where it attains its most extreme sharpness, is not in the last anal-

39. The latter accusation is especially made by Luther in his book *Wider das Papsttum zu Rom, vom Teufel gestiftet* [*Against the Papacy in Rome, Founded by the Devil*], 1545 (*WA* 54, [195-205] 206-99, here 237ff.).

40. *Operationes in Psalmos,* 1519-1521, in *WA* 5, 339, 14.

41. *Wider das Papsttum* (see note 39), in *WA* 54, 233, 12-13.

42. For example *Von dem Papstthum zu Rom wider den hochberühmten Romanisten zu Leipzig,* 1520, in *WA* 6, 322, 8-17; and (see note 39) *WA* 54, 233, 10-14, and 237, 7.

43. *Smalcald Articles* II, 4, 10ff., *BSLK,* 430f.

44. *WA* 54, 229, 28 (see note 39). Luther had judged the historical development similarly already in 1518 in his *Resolutiones disputationum de indulgentiarum virtute* on the ninety-five theses against indulgences (*WA* 1, [522-524] 525-628, here 571).

ysis a *judgment of principle,* but rather a *judgment of fact,* by which Luther says: That's how things are in my time and have been for a very long time; on the basis of these facts I can only make an extremely negative judgment [of the papacy] and also see no possibility that things could really change [for the better] so that my judgment would no longer hold good. Despite that, Luther does not repudiate *any possibility* of a renewed papacy that would have a legitimate task in the church. Even in his last polemically unrestrained anti-papal document *Against the Papacy in Rome, Founded by the Devil* (1545), in which the rejection of the papal ministry seems to become in fact something like a judgment of principle, he speaks of the possibility of an honorary primacy befitting the pope — "der ehren und fürgangs halben" ["for the sake of honor and procedure"] — and an office of supervision "over doctrine and heresy in the church."[45]

46. *Melanchthon's* attitude to the papal ministry was rather similar. Consideration should also be given to Luther's confessional writings, which — with the exception of the *Small Catechism* — admittedly speak critically of the pope and the papal office, but only Luther's *Smalcald Articles* and especially Melanchthon's treatise *De potestate et primatu papae* treat the pope and the papal office as a central theme.

47. In these writings it is striking that the "antichristian" features of the papal office that are allegedly inimical to the gospel are deduced both by Luther and by Melanchthon from its *ius divinum* claim. The *Smalcald Articles* begin this attack and repeat it twice over.[46] This is even more the case in Melanchthon's treatise. All three accusations, as adduced in Luther's "Antichrist" verdict, are — according to the treatise — consequences or implications of the papal *ius divinum* claim:

- the exemption of the pope from all criticism, also criticism from Holy Scripture,
- the power of the pope to introduce new commandments and doctrines binding on the faithful, and
- obedience to the pope as the necessary condition for salvation.[47]

---

45. *Wider das Papsttum* (see note 39) in *WA* 54, 231, 25-28.

46. II, 4, 7 (*BSLK* 429): ". . . dass er nicht iure divino oder aus Gottes Gebot der Oberst wäre. . . ." ["That the Pope is not, according to divine law *(iure divino)* or according to the Word of God, the head of all Christendom . . ."]; cf. II, 4, 12f. (*BSLK* 431). Luther, as is well known, had already questioned the *ius divinum* of the papal ministry in his Leipzig Disputation, 1519 (*WA* 2, [250-53] 254-383).

47. The pope's claim to be "supreme by divine right" (Treatise 5: *BSLK* 472) — according to Melanchthon — also included the claim that he had "the authority to make all kinds of law

48. Seen in this light, the brunt of the critique of the papacy is directed against the implications and consequences of the *ius divinum* claim of the papal ministry. It is important to note the differentiation between a claim of divine right *as such* and that of the implications or consequences that were drawn from it. In the treatise *De potestate et primatu papae* this comes into play in the shift from denouncing the divine-right claim to rejecting the papal claim to infallibility. This amounts to concentrating the argument on what was, in the prevailing understanding, an essential *implication* of the papal claim of *ius divinum*. Undoubtedly Melanchthon in this treatise also places the *ius divinum* claim of papal primacy in question, first on the basis of biblical and historical arguments.[48] He confirms this in his endorsement of Luther's *Smalcald Articles*, where he asserts that the pope only enjoys primacy *iure humano*.[49]

49. Despite that, Melanchthon offers a highly remarkable argument:

> . . . etiamsi Romanus episcopus jure divino haberet primatum, tamen, postquam defendit impios cultus et doctrinam pugnantem cum evangelio, non debetur ei obedientia. Imo necesse est ei tanquam Antichristo adversari.[50]

50. In making this assertion, the treatise appeals not only to Galatians 1:8, but also to canon law, according to which no obedience would be owing to a heretical pope. It enunciates these thoughts also by appealing to the precedent of the Old Testament: for even to the Old Testament high priests, who had incontestably exercised their priesthood wholly *de iure divino,* no obedience was owed as soon as they became godless, as denounced by Jeremiah and other prophets.[51]

---

concerning acts of worship, concerning changing the Sacraments and concerning doctrine" (472; cf. 40: *BSLK* 484). It also included the claim that everything he decreed must "be believed at the peril of forfeiting salvation" (6: *BSLK* 472; cf. 36: *BSLK* 483). And lastly it belongs to the *ius divinum* claim of the Pope that he "does not want to be judged," either by the church (i.e., through a Council: 40: *BSLK* 485; cf. 49: *BSLK* 487) or through Holy Scripture (56: *BSLK* 488).

48. *Treatise* 7-20 (*BSLK* 472-77).

49. See note 52 below.

50. So the Latin text (*BSLK* 488f.). ". . . even if the bishop of Rome had the primacy by divine right (jure divino), yet since he defends godless services and doctrine conflicting with the Gospel, obedience is not due him; yea, it is necessary to resist him as Antichrist." The other statement comes before this: "Even though the bishop of Rome had the primacy and superiority by divine right (divino jure) nevertheless obedience would not be due those pontiffs who defend godless services, idolatry, and doctrine conflicting with the Gospel" (*BSLK* 483).

51. *BSLK* 483f.

51. Even on the supposition that the *ius divinum* claim of the pope might be valid, therefore, it does not follow that one must agree with him and submit in every instance, even if he pronounces a doctrine that contradicts the gospel. Melanchthon wishes to exclude a version of papal authority that attributes to papal decisions a finality that blocks any critical recourse, thereby depriving the scripturally attested gospel of its force as supreme norm. Seen in this light, the Reformation insistence on primacy as a mere "human right" *(de iure humano)* means, in essence and according to its intention, only the firm rejection of a *maximalist interpretation* of the *ius divinum* claim through which the papal ministry evades, or tries to usurp, the norm of the gospel. That means the papal claim of *ius divinum* as such could have remained uncontested, if it were not linked by the Roman school with *implications and aspects* that in the judgment of the reformers deform it by excess and make it the inclusive concept for all the charges. Hence the Lutheran denial of the *ius divinum* of the pope is not a categorical one in principle, but a *"qualified"* rejection.

52. Here too — in much the same way as in Luther — we see a differentiation between the papal ministry as such and an exercise of it that is inimical to the gospel. This differentiation enables us to envisage a renewed Petrine ministry in conformity with the gospel, which would be, even from a Reformation point of view, possible, meaningful, and acceptable. The well-known vote that Melanchthon appended to his signature under the *Smalcald Articles* corresponds to this. In this endorsement Melanchthon recurred to Luther's own conditional affirmation of the papal ministry that Luther, however, had not articulated in his *Smalcald Articles*. Melanchthon explains at the same time what task this conditionally accepted ministry would imply:

> I, Philip Melanchthon, also regard [approve] the above articles as right and Christian. But as to the pope, I hold that, if he would allow the Gospel, we might admit and grant him his superiority over the bishops which he has by human right *(jure humano),* for the sake of the peace and general unity also of those Christians who are under him and may be under him in future.[52]

52. "Ich Philippus Melanthon (!) halt diese obgestallte Artikel auch fur recht und christlich, vom Bapst aber halt ich, so er das Evangelium wollte zulassen, dass ihm umb Friedens und gemeiner Einigkeit willen derjenigen Christen, so auch unter ihm sind und kunftig sein möchten, sein Superiorität uber die Bischofe, die er hat jure humano, auch von uns zuzulassen (und zu geben) sei" (*BSLK* 463f.). Already three years earlier Melanchthon, in a testimonial for Francis I ("De potestate ecclesiastica") had said even more forcibly: "Prodest, iudicio meo illa monarchia Romani Pontificis ad hoc, ut doctrinae consensus retineretur in

2. Developments in Catholic Understanding of the Papal Ministry

53. A reflection on the original, theologically founded papal critique of Luther and the other Lutheran reformers, as described above, offers the chance to come closer to a possible agreement on the Petrine ministry. For the points raised at that time led to the *communio* of the church being broken and to ever-more divergent positions. In fact, in the centuries that followed the Reformation, the papal critique was increasingly systematized and sharpened on the Lutheran side — the expression of growing alienation. In the twentieth century, Lutheran theologians once again returned to the original theological core of Luther's critique. They did so also in the report of the official Lutheran–Roman Catholic dialogue group in the USA in 1974.[53]

54. On the Catholic side, vice versa, a growing intensification of the papal claim to authority has taken place since the Counter-Reformation. This development, however, had already begun in the Middle Ages, especially under Pope Innocent III, who was the first systematically to make an exclusive claim to the title of *vicarius Christi,* in order to provide a theological justification for the *plenitudo potestatis* of the pope. It then culminated in the two dogmas on primacy of jurisdiction and on papal infallibility promulgated by Vatican I in 1870. But in the Catholic Church and in Catholic theology, too, a similar process of recurring to and reflecting on the original *communio* tradition occurred both during and after Vatican II. It was prompted by the needs for church reform and the overcoming of Counter-Reformation unilateralism, and inseparably bound up with a critical and historical reflection on the dogmas of Vatican I. In addition, Vatican II addressed the concerns of the ecumenical movement that had long moved many Lutherans and Catholics.

55. As shown under the analysis of the papal critique of Luther and the other Lutheran reformers, their critique was not directed against the papal ministry as such, to which Luther had accepted a legitimate exercise up to and

---

multis nationibus. Quare facile potest constitui concordia in hoc articulo de superioritate Pontificia, si caeteris articulis conveniri poterit" (*Corpus Reformatorum* 2, 746 [August 1534]); "In my judgment, the benefit of that monarchy of the Roman Pontiff is to maintain doctrinal consensus among many nations. Whence agreement on pontifical superiority can easily be attained, if it shall be the case for the other articles."

53. *Papal Primacy and the Universal Church,* ed. Paul C. Empie and T. Austin Murphy (Minneapolis: Augsburg, 1974); cf. Hans Jörg Urban, "Der reformatorische Protest gegen das Papsttum: Eine theologiegeschichtliche Skizze," in *Petrus und Papst: Evangelium, Einheit der Kirche, Papstdienst,* ed. Albert Brandenburg and Hans Jörg Urban (Münster: Aschendorff, 1977), pp. 266-90.

including Pope Gregory I (590-604). Rather, it was directed against an abusive exercise of that office, through which the pope had raised himself into the lord and judge over the Word of God and the faith of the church. This same distinction between the papal ministry as such and its exercise contrary to the gospel is also found in Melanchthon and in the *Smalcald Articles,* where the roots of the abuse of the papal office are located in the pope's *ius divinum* claim. But here too it can be shown that a *ius divinum* of the papal ministry was not fundamentally repudiated: only its maximalist interpretation, which placed in question the primacy of the gospel, was rejected. Despite the sharpness of their papal critique, and despite the dangerous self-dynamic that their "Antichrist verdict" inevitably generated, among the Lutheran reformers the question about papal primacy, theologically considered, remained curiously open. It remained like a faint, even if largely concealed, hope for a renewed papacy that would satisfy the Reformation concerns and that would never be wholly lost.

56. If this analysis is correct, the individual critical points of the reformers can be understood as hopes and demands whose fulfillment would make possible a recognition of the papal ministry. They were hopes that not only appealed to the gospel, but that ultimately were nourished by basic convictions of the church's tradition that had endured ever since the origins of Christianity through two millennia. Even Vatican I neither wished nor could deny them, and Vatican II expressly made reference to them. These basic convictions include the following:

- that Jesus Christ is and must remain the one Lord, Pastor, and Teacher of the church and the bishops ought to exercise their office of governing the church only on behalf of and following the example of Christ, namely as *vicarii Christi;*
- that — in opposition to the exclusive claim of Innocent III and his followers — all bishops are *vicarii Christi* for their local churches and bear responsibility for the whole church and its fidelity to the faith in common with the successor of Peter;
- that the church as a whole is promised the aid of the Holy Spirit in preserving the gospel in inerring fidelity to the faith;
- that therefore the unanimous witness of the whole believing and teaching church is the proper means of ascertaining the true faith, and this witness, if necessary, is to be given in councils and synods, whose doctrinal decisions are confirmed by their ensuing approbation and acceptance (now termed "reception") in the local churches;

- that the Holy Scripture, the Word of God and witness of faith of the apostles, is the supreme guideline for the faith and teaching of the church.

57. The recognition that Luther and other reformers accorded to Pope Gregory I as the "last bishop of Rome" is clear evidence that their papal critique received important impulses from this tradition. For it was this pope who had rejected the title of an *universalis episcopus* that had been offered to him, and who had at the same time emphasized the dignity of his fellow-bishops as *vicarii Christi* and professed his primacy over the whole church as "servant of the servants of God": "My honor is the honor of the whole Church. My honor is the firm strength of my brothers. I am truly honored, when due honor is paid to each and every one." Even Vatican I made a point of citing this declaration of the pope (ND 827; DH 3061). In fact the exclusive claim — founded on an alleged *ius divinum* — of the popes since Innocent III to the title of *vicarius Christi*, an exclusivity that Gregory I had nevertheless rejected, was the real theological basis for an exaggerated claim to authority on the part of the popes and for the affirmation of Roman centralism. This the reformers saw aright.

58. A certain image of the church, based on this commonly shared tradition, namely that of the brotherly communion of the people of God, as grounded in the preaching of Jesus, in the images of the Bible, and in the practice of the early church, plainly also plays a part in the reformers' critique of the papal claims. Criticism of the fact that bishops and pope had increasingly come to resemble worldly princes in their lordly claims and sumptuous lifestyle, that they had confused the exercise of spiritual power and worldly power, and thus obscured the original form of the church, was not limited just to the reformers. It runs through the whole of church history, and repeatedly gave rise to reform movements. It is no accident that the Franciscan movement, which wanted to live a life of poverty and brotherhood in the *sequela Christi*, made headway just in the time of Innocent III.

59. On the other hand, it was this same Innocent III who gave an acknowledged status in the church to the poverty movement in the shape of the mendicant orders, against the resistance of the bishops. In fact it was not only the popes' thirst for power that led to their heightened claims to authority. In not a few cases these claims were put forward so as to be able to push through reforms in the church and resist the aims of worldly rulers who wanted to subject the church to their administration (investiture controversy). Accusations continued within the Catholic Church that the papal primacy had taken on the pretensions of an all-inclusive sovereignty both inside and outside the

church, all the way down to the First Vatican Council. At this Council objections were raised against the draft text. It was accused of presenting papal primacy too much according to a kind of worldly model of rule and as the absolute monarchy of the pope. The ordinary and immediate jurisdiction of the bishops as *vicarii Christi* for their local churches was, it was claimed, jeopardized by this idea. This became one of the main concerns of the minority bishops at Vatican I.

60. These brief references to the multilayered nature of the history of the church and of the papacy, and the previous analysis of the papal critique of the reformers, show how much the concerns of the Protestant reformers in their critique of the papacy, and those made within the Catholic Church itself, have in common on the basis of their commonly shared tradition — a communion that could form the basis for a possible ecumenical understanding. The explosive force that the Reformation critique of the pope and church eventually released, leading to schism, as well as the reaction of the Catholic Church to it, nearly consigned the reality of this common heritage to oblivion.

61. This common heritage seemed to have disappeared at last with Vatican I. For with its two dogmas on the papal office this Council seemed finally to set its seal on the sovereign status of the pope that had hitherto been contested on theological grounds even by Catholics. This impression was reinforced not only among non-Catholics. Many ultramontanist Catholics hailed the fact that the previously long and cumbersome process of establishing truth within the church through synods and councils had — so they opined — become superfluous. In the face of the onslaught of Modernism, hostile alike to church and faith, it seemed to them that a bastion of undeniable certainty had thereby been won for the faith and security for the church. Both dogmas, on the primacy of jurisdiction and on the infallible teaching office of the pope, were interpreted to Catholics along exactly these lines. Anyone who ventures on the path toward an ecumenical understanding of the papal ministry cannot avoid having to recognize the effect of Vatican I as one of the most important obstacles on this path.

Chapter II

Vatican I on Papacy *(Pastor Aeternus)*

A. The Infallible Teaching Office of the Pope

1. The Dogma

62. In connection with the pope's primacy of jurisdiction, the "infallible teaching authority of the Roman Pontiff" is treated in chapter IV of Vatican I's Dogmatic Constitution *Pastor aeternus.*[1] The pope's supreme teaching authority is here presented as part of his apostolic primacy as successor of Peter, not as part of his primacy of jurisdiction. It is described as *suprema magisterii potestas,* the supreme power of teaching (ND 831; DH 3065). The differentiation of the primacy of teaching from the primacy of jurisdiction, the other form of expression of the Petrine primacy, takes into account the complex nature of the primacy of teaching. It is the supreme power to present a teaching as testimony of the revelation transmitted in Holy Scripture and in the faith and teaching of the church and to declare this teaching as binding and obligatory for the church as a whole. So the pope's supreme power is twofold in nature: it is both one of witness and one of jurisdiction.

63. As can be understood from the section of the Constitution introducing the definition (ND 839/1; DH 3073) and the canon that concludes chapter IV

1. On the following, see the most comprehensive study on Vatican Council I, that of Klaus Schatz, *Vaticanum I: 1869-1870,* 3 vols. (Paderborn: Schöningh, 1992-1994). Regarding the historical and theological presuppositions of the definition of papal infallibility, see also Hermann Josef Pottmeyer, *Unfehlbarkeit und Souveränität: Die päpstliche Unfehlbarkeit im System der ultramontanen Ekklesiologie des 19. Jahrhunderts* (Mainz: Matthias-Grünewald-Verlag, 1975).

(ND 840; DH 3075), the last paragraph of the chapter (ND 839/2; DH 3074) contains the real definition of the dogma. It reads as follows:

> It is a divinely revealed dogma that the Roman Pontiff, when he speaks *ex cathedra,* that is, when, acting in the office of shepherd and teacher of all Christians, he defines, by virtue of his supreme apostolic authority, a doctrine concerning faith or morals to be held by the universal church, possesses through the divine assistance promised to him in the person of Blessed Peter, the infallibility with which the divine Redeemer willed his church to be endowed in defining the doctrine concerning faith or morals; and that such definitions of the Roman Pontiff are therefore irreformable of themselves, not because of the consent of the church *(ex sese, non autem ex consensu ecclesiae).*[2]

2. *Hermeneutics of the Dogma*

64. An interpretation of the dogma must necessarily start out from the wording of the dogmatic definition itself. Chapter IV of the Constitution, in which the definition is placed, and the Constitution as a whole, reveal the definition's wider connotation. Indications on the Council's purpose in issuing this dogma can further be deduced from the pronouncements of the responsible conciliar Commission, its reactions and responses to the proposals and objections of the Council Fathers, and its explanations of the meaning of individual formulations of the Constitution. Lastly, the conciliar debate itself also provides information on the aims and concerns of the Council Fathers who influenced the formulation of the dogma.

3. *The Content of the Dogma*

65. A decision issued *ex cathedra* — the technical term adopted by the Council for the infallible dogmatic pronouncements of the pope — differs

---

2. "Romanum Pontificem, cum ex cathedra loquitur, id est, cum omnium Christianorum pastoris et doctoris munere fungens pro suprema sua Apostolica auctoritate doctrinam de fide vel moribus ab universa Ecclesia tenendam definit, per assistentiam divinam ipsi in beato Petro promissam, ea infallibilitate pollere, qua divinus Redemptor Ecclesiam suam in definienda doctrina de fide vel moribus instructam esse voluit; ideoque eiusmodi Romani Pontificis definitiones ex sese, non autem ex consensu Ecclesiae, irreformabiles esse."

from other papal doctrinal pronouncements in terms of subject, object, and act.

66. An *ex cathedra* decision differs as far as its *subject* is concerned: a decision by the pope is only infallible "when, acting in the office of shepherd and teacher of all Christians, he defines, by virtue of his supreme apostolic authority," a doctrine concerning faith or morals (ND 839/2; DH 3074). As the spokesman of the responsible Commission, Bishop Gasser, observed on this point, infallibility belongs to the pope not as a private teacher, but as *persona publica,* that is, as earthly head and supreme teacher of the church and hence in his relation to the universal church.[3]

67. The formulation *when he defines* makes it clear — according to Gasser — that infallibility is no habitual quality of the pope, but is limited to only such pronouncements in which he appeals to his supreme authority as successor of Peter. Gasser further explained that the pope did not enjoy the privilege of infallibility in general by virtue of his office, but only insofar as he received God's assistance in these particular acts.[4] In order to make it plain that infallibility was not a habitual quality of the papal office, the original title of chapter IV *De Romanorum pontificum infallibilitate* was replaced by the formulation *De Romani Pontificis infallibili magisterio.*[5]

68. An *ex cathedra* decision differs as far as its *object* is concerned: infallibility is only accorded to the papal office of teaching in the definition of a *doctrine concerning faith or morals* (ND 839/2; DH 3074). This is further explained in chapter IV:

> For the Holy Spirit was not promised to the successors of Peter that they might disclose a new doctrine by his revelation, but rather, that, with his assistance, they might jealously guard and faithfully explain the revelation or deposit of faith that was handed down through the apostles.[6]

3. *Mansi* 52, 1212f.: "Infallibilitas personalis papae in se ipsa debet accuratius definiri, quod nempe non competit Romano pontifici quatenus est persona privata, neque etiam quatenus est doctor privatus, . . . sed quatenus est persona Romani pontificis, seu persona publica, id est, caput ecclesiae in sua relatione ad ecclesiam universalem."

4. *Mansi* 52, 1213 AB: "Neque etiam dicendus est pontifex infallibilis simpliciter ex auctoritate papatus, sed ut subest divinae assistentiae dirigenti in hoc certe et indubie. . . . Hinc sententia: Romanus pontifex est infallibilis . . . est solummodo incompleta, cum papa solummodo est infallibilis quando solemni iudicio pro universa ecclesia res fidei et morum definit."

5. *Mansi* 52, 1218 D.

6. *ND* 836. "Neque enim Petri successoribus Spiritus Sanctus promissus est, ut eo revelante novam doctrinam patefacerent, sed ut, eo assistente traditam per Apostolos revelationem seu fidei depositum sancte custodirent et fideliter exponerent" (*DH* 3070).

69. By its limitation to revealed truths, the normative character of the apostolic transmission of the revelation is thus underlined. By the same token, the assumption that the pope was the sole beneficiary of a special revelation or divine inspiration as the reason for his infallibility is excluded. Papal infallibility is based instead on the assistance of the Holy Spirit, which is promised both to Peter, with a view to maintaining the church in the true faith, and to the believing church as a whole. The infallibility of the papal teaching office is participation in that infallibility — as the definition of the dogma puts it — "with which the divine Redeemer willed his church to be endowed in defining the doctrine concerning faith or morals" (ND 839/2; DH 3074).

70. An *ex cathedra* decision differs as far as its *act* is concerned: the pope only speaks infallibly when he decides that "a doctrine concerning faith or morals [is] to be held by the universal Church" (ND 839/2; DH 3074). An *ex cathedra* decision should therefore — as Gasser's commentary underlines — be differentiated not only from the pope's private pronouncements, but also from those doctrinal affirmations which the pope presents in his role as supreme teacher of the church, but which he does not wish to make obligatory for the faithful in a binding and definitive manner. In *ex cathedra* decisions the pope must explicitly spell out that it is his intention to pronounce a definitive judgment and that the doctrine in question is to be observed by the whole church.[7]

71. The definition ends with the sentence: ". . . such definitions of the Roman Pontiff are therefore irreformable of themselves, not because of the consent of the Church" (ND 839; DH 3074). The formulation *of themselves* was supplemented immediately before the final vote with the addendum *not because of the consent of the church,* without any previous examination or discussion of this additional clause by the Council. It was this procedure that caused the departure of the minority bishops before the final vote on the dogma.

72. This addendum in effect gives the impression that the idea of an infallibility of the pope detached from, or independent of, the church had gained acceptance at the Council. On the basis of this impression, the addendum indeed took on a momentous significance in the period after the Council.

---

7. *Mansi* 52, 1225 BC: "Quando summus pontifex loquitur ex cathedra, primo non tamquam doctor privatus, neque solum tamquam episcopus ac ordinarius alicuius diocesis vel provinciae aliquid decernit, sed docet supremi omnium christianorum pastoris et doctoris munere fungens. Secundo non sufficit quivis modus proponendi doctrinam, etiam dum pontifex fungitur munere supremi pastoris et doctoris, sed requiritur intentio manifesta definiendi doctrinam . . . tenendam ab ecclesia universali."

Outside the Catholic Church the rejection of this dogma appealed to it. Inside the Catholic Church, it lent verisimilitude to the maximalist interpretation of the dogma, which was gaining ground in catechesis and theology. At a time when the Catholic Church felt herself, both spiritually and politically, to be in a state of siege, the infallible pope seemed to her the last bastion against the advancing tide of faithlessness by which she felt herself assailed. Playing down the conditions and limitations cited in the definition, the maximalist interpretation made the infallibility of the pope appear as the very foundation and source of the church's infallibility in faith and in doctrine. This went together with the simultaneous maximalist interpretation of the dogma of the papal primacy of jurisdiction.

73. The addendum also made plain the anti-Gallican thrust of the definition. Like the definition as a whole, its intention was to exclude the doctrine of Gallicanism: more precisely, to exclude the notion that the formal assent of the episcopate or of the church was an essential prerequisite for any *ex cathedra* decision to be accepted as irreformable and free of error. This doctrine had led in France to a situation in which Roman doctrinal pronouncements and judgments had little effect, or were ignored, as a result of Gallican claims that they lacked approval by the church, as was the case for instance in the Jansenist conflict. Gallicanism, besides, had degenerated into an ideology that demanded the church's dependence on sovereign state power.

74. In substance, however, the addendum does not alter the sense of the definition. Gasser pointed this out. The addendum, he said, expressed in a negative form the same concept that the expression *of themselves* expressed in a positive form, namely, that the irreformability of an *ex cathedra* decision is exclusively and solely founded in the special mission given to Peter by Christ and Christ's promise to Peter and in the corresponding divine assistance, which preserves the pope from error in making such a decision for the sake of the truth of the faith professed by the church.[8]

75. In spite of this apt explanation by Gasser, the addendum to the definition does seem to have a theologically misleading effect, as the maximalist interpretation shows. It can, in other words, be manipulated to suggest a mu-

---

8. *Mansi* 52, 1317 AB: "Nam reapse cum dicimus, definitiones Romani pontificis ex cathedra loquentis esse irreformabiles ex sese, eo ipso enuntiamus causam irreformabilitatis sitam esse in ipsis decretis Romani pontificis, et non esse ponendam aliunde ex conditione quadam externa, ut est assensus episcoporum, assensus ecclesiae. Ergo haec verba nihil aliud continent nisi ulteriorem quandam explicationem, ut eandem rem primo dicamus positive et deinde negative. . . . 'Huiusmodi definitiones Romani pontificis irreformabiles esse ex sese, non autem ex consensu ecclesiae.'"

tually exclusive opposition between divine assistance and the cooperation of the church in the establishment of the truth: but no such opposition exists or had been intended by the Council.

4. Did the Council Teach an Absolute, Personal, and Separate Infallibility of the Pope?

76. While the above-cited addendum does enable us to recognize the definition's anti-Gallican thrust, its anti-Gallican tendency has had a far unhappier — because concealed — effect: namely, by preventing the minority from introducing into the conciliar text any mention of the need for appropriate cooperation of the church in the establishment of the truth. The Council closed its ears to this wish, because it feared lest any such mention would offer Gallicanism a pretext for placing in question the authority of *ex cathedra* decisions by alleging lack of consultation. Even more so than the above-cited addendum, this silence about the dependence of the pope on the support of the church in the establishment of the truth helped to promote the maximalist interpretation of the dogma. That interpretation was concerned solely with the pope's sovereign power of decision that seemed to exclude any reciprocity in the relation between pope and church. That the Council did not at all wish to repudiate this dependence of the pope can only be inferred from the conciliar debate, and especially from the pronouncements of the responsible Commission chaired by Bishop Gasser.

77. With regard to this silence, the Council Fathers of the minority warned against the definition of an absolute, personal, and separate infallibility of the pope — a conception they had detected in the preliminary drafts. His infallibility, they argued, would seem *absolute,* if an *ex cathedra* decision be unconditional; *personal,* if it be exclusively dependent on the pope, his will, and his knowledge, as suggested by a personal inspiration of the pope; and *separate,* if it be reached without any involvement of the episcopate and church in the establishment of the truth. The argument over these three accusations formed the core of the conciliar debate.

78. As regards the accusation of an *absolute* infallibility, thanks to it the minority did succeed in contributing to a clarification of the conditions of an *ex cathedra* decision. Gasser made the following observation on this:

> Absolute infallibility only belongs to God, the first and essential truth, who can never deceive nor in any way be deceived. Since all other infallibility is

conferred for a particular purpose, it has limitations and conditions, on the basis of which its claims can be judged.[9]

79. As regards the accusation of a *personal* infallibility, we may cite the already-mentioned remarks of Gasser, namely, that infallibility was granted to the pope neither as a private person, nor as a habitual quality of the papal office, nor on the grounds of any particular revelation vouchsafed to him. Infallibility could only be called personal, insofar as it is promised to the pope in virtue of his office and for particular acts, but not to the local Church of Rome or to the Apostolic See, as the Gallicans maintained.[10]

80. The most important accusation of the minority, however, was ultimately aimed at showing that the text laid before the Council Fathers attributed a *separate* infallibility to the pope. In other words, it remained silent about the need to involve or consult the church in the establishment of the truth. Here the different interests of majority and minority clashed. Mindful of the risk of Gallicanism, the majority wanted to avoid any such mention, whereas for the minority a dogma was above all the authentic witness of the revealed truth and faith of the church. In the view of the minority, primacy was admittedly given to Peter and was not divisible; but as attestation of the truth his decision, like any witness, would gain in persuasiveness through the consent of many witnesses; that is why, since time immemorial, synods and councils were *par excellence* the appropriate place for the establishment of the truth and for doctrinal decisions. It is not hard to recognize that in these disputes a role was played not only by conflicting interests, but also by the complex nature of the teaching office itself: being, on the one side, an authority of jurisdiction or *potestas,* and on the other, an authority of witness.

81. In concrete terms, the minority, in its arguments, started out from the presupposition that since the pope is not divinely inspired, it follows that he

9. *Mansi* 52, 1214 A: "Nullo in sensu infallibilitas pontificia est absoluta, nam infallibilitas absoluta competit soli Deo, primae et essentiali veritati, qui nullibi et numquam fallere nec falli potest. Omnis alia infallibilitas utpote communicata ad certum finem habet suos limites et suas conditiones, sub quibus adesse censetur."

10. *Mansi* 52, 1212 C: "Dicenda est personalis ut sic excludatur distinctio inter Romanum pontificem et Romanam ecclesiam. Porro infallibilitas dicitur personalis, ut sic excludatur distinctio inter sedem et sedentem. Cum haec distinctio in congregationibus generalibus nullos nacta fuerit patronos, etiam de iis aliquid addendo supersedeo. Reiecta ergo distinctione inter ecclesiam Romanam et Romanum pontificem, inter sedem et sedentem, id est, inter seriem universam et inter singulos Romanos pontifices in hac serie sibi succedentes, defendimus personalem Romani pontificis infallibilitatem eatenus, quatenus haec praerogativa omnibus et singulis legitimis Petri in cathedra eius successoribus ex Christi promissione competit."

is dependent on human means when seeking the truth. The most suitable means to this end, the minority argued, was the cooperation of the bishops in the truth-finding process. In a comparable way shepherds and teachers in the church bear witness to the faith of their particular churches and share collegial joint responsibility for the whole church.

82. In its response, the responsible commission repeatedly and exhaustively examined this concern of the minority. It acknowledged that the use of human means indeed belonged to the establishment of the truth. The pope thus had the moral obligation to inform himself conscientiously about the faith of the church through Scripture and Tradition and through the bishops or in other ways. This, said the commission, was a normal, indeed necessary procedure.[11] This position was vehemently underlined by Gasser.[12] This self-evident moral obligation of the pope, however, should not, according to the commission, be part of the definition, nor ought the ways and means of consultation be explicitly articulated, since they necessarily depend on prevailing conditions. Above all, the need for such consultation, which in any case could not be strict and absolute, should not be understood as the condition for the validity of an *ex cathedra* decision — a condition that was wrongly derived from the divine constitution of the church. For it followed from Luke 22:32 that Peter should strengthen his brethren in the faith. That is why a special and exclusive privilege, the *charisma veritatis,* is given to him. Only in this sense could one speak of a separate infallibility. But his privilege did not separate the pope from the church. For on the grounds of the divine assistance promised to Peter, one ought to trust that the pope would not proceed arbitrarily, nor would the consent of the church ever be lacking in his decision.[13]

11. *Mansi* 52, 763 D–764 D: "Quare neque diligentiam neque curas potest omittere, quae necessario ad cognoscendam veritatem praerequiruntur. Idcirco papa inquisitionem instituit sive cum clero et theologis ecclesiae Romanae, sive cum formali synodo romana, ut inquirat quid in subiecta fidei et morum materia teneat ecclesia Romana, in qua immaculata semper est servata apostolica doctrina."

12. *Mansi* 52, 1213 CD: "Non separamus porro papam infallibiliter definientem a cooperatione et concursu ecclesiae, saltem id est in eo sensu, quod hanc cooperationem et hunc concursum ecclesiae non excludimus . . . , quia infallibilitas pontificis Romani non per modum inspirationis vel revelationis, sed per modum divinae assistentiae ipsi obvenit. Hinc papa pro officio suo et rei gravitate tenetur media apta adhibere ad veritatem rite indagandam et apte enuntiandam; et eiusmodi media sunt concilia vel etiam consilia episcoporum, cardinalium, theologorum etc. Haec media pro diversitate rerum utique sunt diversa, et pie debemus credere quod in divina assistentia Petro et successoribus eius a Christo Domino facta, simul etiam contineatur promissio mediorum, quae necessaria aptaque ad affirmandum infallibile pontificis iudicium."

13. *Mansi* 52, 765 C; 1213f.; 1216 A–1217 A.

83. All these arguments in support of the silence criticized by the minority, however, did not affect, nor remove, a particular concern that was raised by the minority and that referred to the credibility of *ex cathedra* decisions. How could the pope's claim to testify to the faith of the church by his decision be credible, if the church as a public body could not ascertain how he had established the truth of this faith? This concern could once again be best addressed by the involvement of the episcopate in the establishment of the truth. Gasser himself described the relation between pope and church as a *publica relatio,* which consequently was subject to public conditions.

84. The explanations made in the name of the commission show that it could not wholly exclude the justified concerns of the minority. But since the anti-Gallican thrust precluded any corresponding mention of them in the definition itself, the commission decided to adopt the following text in chapter IV:

> [T]he Roman Pontiffs, according as the conditions of the times and the circumstances dictated, sometimes by calling together ecumenical Councils or sounding out the mind of the Church throughout the world, sometimes through regional Councils, or sometimes by using other helps which divine Providence supplied, have defined as having to be held those matters which, with the help of God, they had found consonant with the Holy Scriptures and with the apostolic Traditions.[14]

85. While the inclusion of this text in the Constitution was a success of the minority, it was not enough to satisfy it. The text does not speak of any need for an appropriate cooperation of episcopate and church. Moreover, it refers only to past practice. The question remained whether the earlier practice should also determine future practice — a question that many bishops of the minority considered crucial if they were to give their final assent to the dogma. Here a book by Bishop Fessler of St. Pölten, Secretary of the Council, came to their help. It was published shortly after the Council. It explained that this text was essential for the interpretation of the dogma, because the popes would act in this way also in future.[15] What was decisive in this sense, how-

---

14. "Romani autem Pontifices, prout temporum et rerum condicio suadebat, nunc convocatis oecumenicis Conciliis aut explorata Ecclesiae per orbem dispersae sententia, nunc per Synodos particulares, nunc aliis, quae divina suppeditabat providentia, adhibitis auxiliis, ea tenenda definiverunt, quae sacris Scripturis et apostolicis traditionibus consentanea, Deo adiutore, cognoverant" (*ND* 835; *DH* 3069).

15. See Joseph Fessler, *Die wahre und die falsche Unfehlbarkeit der Päpste: Zur Abwehr gegen Hrn. Prof. Dr. Schulte* (Vienna: Sartori, 1871), p. 21.

ever, was the fact that Fessler received a letter from Pius IX, in which the pope declared that Fessler in his book had placed the real sense of the dogma in its true light.[16]

86. In short: The explanations made in the name of the responsible Commission make it clear that the definition's silence about the duty incumbent on the pope to seek consultation, its appropriateness and principal need, and the subsidiary character of *ex cathedra* decisions, do not signify any rejection of such concerns. But the silence has all the same helped to promote the maximalist interpretation of the dogma, which for its part corresponded to a further extension of the primacy of jurisdiction and reinforced this development. That Pius XII proclaimed the dogma of the Assumption of Mary in 1950 as an *ex cathedra* decision contradicted Gasser's references to the subsidiary character of such decisions. There is no doubt, however, that Vatican I left in place the pope's absolute binding relationship to the witnesses of the revelation and to the faith of the church that is founded on them.

5. The Dogma in the Second Vatican Council

87. Vatican II took over the dogma of Vatican I unchanged. However, it did place emphases that dissolved the basis of the maximalist interpretation of the dogma. It thus took over from the *Acta* of Vatican I Gasser's reference to the pope's duty to engage in a conscientious procedure for the establishment of the truth. It further cited, together with the supreme teaching authority of the pope, also that of the college of bishops and its infallibility — a theme that Vatican I could no longer tackle. Thus, the Dogmatic Constitution on the Church *Lumen gentium* contains the following pronouncements:

> Furthermore, when the Roman Pontiff, or the body of bishops together with him, define a doctrine, they do so in conformity with revelation itself, by which all are bound to abide and to which they are obliged to conform; and this revelation is transmitted in its entirety either in written form or in oral tradition through the legitimate succession of bishops and above all through the care of the Roman Pontiff himself; and through the light of the Spirit of truth it is scrupulously preserved in the church and unerringly explained. The Roman Pontiff and the bishops, in virtue of their office and

16. See Klaus Schatz, *Vaticanum I: 1869-1870*, vol. 3 (Paderborn: Schöningh, 1994), p. 297.

because of the seriousness of the matter, are assiduous in examining this revelation by every suitable means and in expressing it properly; they do not, however, admit any new public revelation as pertaining to the divine deposit of faith.[17]

The infallibility promised to the church is also present in the body of bishops when, together with Peter's successor, they exercise the supreme teaching office.[18]

88. In addition, Vatican II took over Gasser's explanatory remarks on the controversial addendum to the definition of the dogma *"and not because of the consent of the Church,"* as follows:

For that reason, his [the pope's] definitions are rightly said to be irreformable by their very nature and not by reason of the consent of the church, inasmuch as they were made with the assistance of the holy Spirit promised to him in blessed Peter; and as a consequence they are not in need of the approval of others and do not admit of appeal to any other tribunal. For in such a case, the Roman Pontiff does not deliver a pronouncement as a private person, but rather does he expound and defend the teaching of the catholic faith as the supreme teacher of the universal church, in whom, as an individual, the charism of infallibility of the church itself is present.[19]

---

17. "Cum autem sive Romanus Pontifex sive Corpus Episcoporum cum eo sententiam definiunt, eam proferunt secundum ipsam Revelationem, cui omnes stare et conformari tenentur et quae scripta vel tradita per legitimam Episcoporum successionem et imprimis ipsius Romani Pontificis cura integre transmittitur, atque praelucente Spiritu veritatis in Ecclesia sancte servatur et fideliter exponitur. Ad quam rite indagandam et apte enuntiandam, Romanus Pontifex et Episcopi, pro officio suo et rei gravitate, per media apta, sedulo operam navant; novam vero revelationem publicam tamquam ad divinum fidei depositum pertinentem non accipiunt" (*LG* 25; *DH* 4150; ET here and following as in VCII, 34-36).

18. "Infallibilitas Ecclesiae promissa in corpore Episcoporum quoque inest, quando supremum magisterium cum Petri Successore exercet" (*LG* 25; *DH* 4150).

19. "Quare definitiones eius ex sese, et non ex consensu ecclesiae, irreformabiles merito dicuntur, quippe quae sub assistentia Spiritus sancti, ipsi in beato Petro promissa, prolatae sint, ideoque nulla indigeant aliorum approbatione, nec ullam ad aliud iudicium appellationem patiantur. Tunc enim Romanus pontifex non ut persona privata sententiam profert, sed ut universalis ecclesiae magister supremus, in quo charisma infallibilitatis ipsius ecclesiae singulariter inest, doctrinam fidei catholicae exponit vel tuetur" (*LG* 25; *DH* 4149).

89. It is striking, however, that Vatican II did not take over Gasser's ensuing remarks on the inherent, even if not indispensable, need for the consultation of the episcopate and church, as well as the subsidiary character of *ex cathedra* decisions.

90. Lastly, Vatican II also took over the following remark of Gasser:

> The assent of the church can never be lacking to such definitions on account of the same holy Spirit's influence, through which Christ's whole flock is maintained in the unity of the faith and makes progress in it.[20]

91. This assurance is given particular weight by the fact that the Council attributes to the concurrence of the whole People of God in matters of faith an infallibility of its own corresponding to the infallibility of the pope's teaching office. This infallibility is based on the *sensus fidelium* of the people of God that is "aroused and sustained by the Spirit of truth." In this earlier passage of the same Constitution it is said, indeed, that the whole body of the faithful cannot err in matters of belief *(in credendo falli nequit).* This characteristic is shown when they, bishops and laity together, manifest their universal consent in matters of faith and morals (cf. LG 12; DH 4130).

92. Since Catholic theology has never excluded the possibility of a heretical pope, the assurance of Gasser and Vatican Council II that an *ex cathedra* decision would never lack universal consent has led leading theologians — one of whom would become pope, two others cardinals — to express the view that the formal refusal of assent on the part of the episcopate and of the whole church would signify that an *ex cathedra* decision in such a case would not, or only apparently, exist.[21] The question whether a reservation about such a decision's compulsory nature would consequently exist and be justified, as deduced from the pope's absolute binding to the witnesses of the revelation and to the faith of the church, merits attention. For a qualified opposition of the whole church would have to appeal to just this binding

20. "Istis autem definitionibus assensus Ecclesiae numquam deesse potest propter actionem eiusdem Spiritus sancti, qua universus Christi grex in unitate fidei servatur et proficit" (*LG* 25; DH 4149).

21. See Joseph Ratzinger, *Das neue Volk Gottes: Entwürfe zur Ekklesiologie* (Düsseldorf: Patmos Verlag, 1969), p. 144; Walter Kasper, "Zur Diskussion um das Problem der Unfehlbarkeit," in *Fehlbar? Eine Bilanz,* ed. Hans Küng (Zürich: Benziger Verlag, 1973), pp. 74-89, here p. 84; Avery Dulles, *A Church to Believe In: Discipleship and the Dynamics of Freedom* (New York: Crossroad, 1982, 1987), p. 139.

relationship. It is worth pointing out, in this connection, that the criteriological role that was attributed to the church's reception of conciliar doctrinal decisions in the first millennium has attracted the attention of postconciliar theology.[22]

B. The Universal Jurisdiction of the Pope

93. Before Vatican I, for complex reasons, doctrinal and historical, objections to the papacy from other churches seemed insurmountable. With the dogma of the universal jurisdiction of the pope, these objections, essentially of an ecclesiological nature, became more insurmountable than ever, even in the eyes of the Orthodox, as in the course of the discussions Bishop Papp-Szilagyi had already predicted: "The Orientals refuse as heretical such a system of government where the pope is an absolute monarch without limitations."[23]

94. Vatican I promulgated that dogma in the following terms:

[I]f anyone says that the Roman Pontiff has only the office of inspection and direction, but not the full and supreme power of jurisdiction over the whole Church, not only in matters that pertain to faith and morals but also in matters that pertain to the discipline and government of the Church throughout the whole world; or if anyone says that he has only a more important part and not the complete fulness of this supreme power; or if anyone says that this power is not ordinary and immediate either over each and every Church or over each and every shepherd and faithful, *anathema sit.*[24]

22. See the article on "Rezeption," in *LThK,* 3rd ed., vol. 8 (Freiburg, Basel, Vienna: Herder, 1999), pp. 1147-52.

23. *Mansi* 52, 310 B: "Hinc systema de absoluta et irrestricta monarchia papae respuunt tamquam haereticum."

24. "Si quis itaque dixerit, Romanum Pontificem habere tantummodo officium inspectionis vel directionis, non autem plenam et supremam potestatem iurisdictionis in universam Ecclesiam, non solum in rebus, quae ad fidem et mores, sed etiam in iis, quae ad disciplinam et regimen Ecclesiae per totum orbem diffusae pertinent; aut eum habere tantum potiores partes, non vero totam plenitudinem huius supremae potestatis; aut hanc eius potestatem non esse ordinariam et immediatam sive in omnes ac singulas ecclesias sive in omnes et singulos pastores et fideles: anathema sit" (*ND* 830; *DH* 3064).

95. This understanding of the universal jurisdiction is therefore a major — if not *the* major — obstacle to a rapprochement between the Catholic Church and other churches. It explains why the Joint International Commission for Theological Dialogue between the Roman Catholic Church and the Orthodox Church has chosen to discuss universal jurisdiction before infallibility. Rightly so, because we are faced here with a basic ecclesiological question: Is it theologically correct to understand the communion of the church, without simultaneously stating that this communion is a communion of churches (in the plural)? This is, however, what Vatican I appears to do, and on this basis one would not easily reach an ecumenical consensus.

96. The dialogue on the Roman primacy must reckon with prejudices. In the beginning of the last century, some Anglicans forged a still timely expression of the problem, to wit: "united, not absorbed." That this suggestion is compatible with the dogma of 1870 may be shown in four stages:

1. Vatican I treated the primacy without any explicit link to the communion of the churches *(communio ecclesiarum)*, whereas today's Catholic interpretation recognizes the internal and external limitations of such an approach.
2. Vatican II rectified the maximalist doctrinal understanding of Vatican I; this has had, however, little effect in matters of discipline.
3. The more representative Catholic theology has integrated the Roman primacy into a frame of a community of churches.
4. The Catholic Church has to engage in shaping a new canonical approach and fill out her hermeneutic of dogma with regard to the Roman primacy.

1. The Universal Jurisdiction of the Pope — Content and Qualifications

97. For half a century, Catholic theologians have been conscious of the many limitations stemming from the wording of the definition of Vatican I that essentially resulted from dealing with Roman primacy without explicit relation to the community of churches. This becomes evident in the vocabulary adopted, as well as in the general structuring of the whole.

98. The vocabulary used for the definition of papal jurisdiction has given rise to many misunderstandings regarding the relationship to other bishops and the statute of the church. The definitions of Vatican I with regard to the

pope's jurisdiction are expressed in a vocabulary that is highly technical. Even Catholics, whether for or against the definition, have often given it a wrong interpretation.[25]

99. Vatican I ascribes *ordinary power* to the pope, which — however — requires a more comprehensive explanation. Before the Fathers' vote, Msgr. Zinelli, speaking on behalf of the Deputation of the Faith, clearly explained that the word *ordinary* is to be understood uniquely in the sense in which it is understood in canon law:

> All legal consultants, all Doctors of Canon Law, all ecclesiastical authors make a distinction between ordinary power and delegated power. For all, *ordinary power* is that which belongs to someone by reason of his charge; *delegated power* is that which is exercised on behalf of another person, in whose case it is *ordinary*. This explanation of terms is sufficient.[26]

25. Already at Vatican I, the bishop of Mainz, von Ketteler, regretted the choice of terms that would give rise to misunderstandings, even questioning whether that choice might not have been intentional: "The entire treatment of the doctrine of primacy gives rise to the suspicion that the intention was never to provide an exact and genuine description of the Church . . . but rather to maximize, in all times and in all places, the authority of the See of Rome which, though it is indeed very holy, is not the only authority in the church. Likewise ambiguous terms and expressions are used which can certainly be given precise interpretations, but which could quite easily be misunderstood and taken to mean . . . on one hand, that the rights of bishops are being denied and, on the other, that authority is being attributed to the Roman Pontiff which belongs to Christ himself. To be sure no one intends that. . . . But then why not state things in such a way as to prevent any possibility of misinterpreting the texts?" (*Mansi* 52, 208 D–209 A: "Tota enim expositio de primatu talis est, ut in lectore sponte provocet suspicionem credendi, non fuisse intentionem doctrinam de ecclesia germano et nativo sensu ac splendido ac harmonico modo exponere; sed eo potius omnia studia tendere, ut auctoritas primae sedis, quae utique sanctissima sed tamen non unica est auctoritas in ecclesia, semper et ubique ad extremum usque audiatur. Simul etiam verba adhibentur ancipitia, quae quidem rectum sensum admittunt, sed facillime etiam praepostere intelligi possent, atque adversariis nostris ansam praebere inde colligendi divina iura episcoporum negata et Romano pontifici dominium attributum esse, quod soli auctori ecclesiae Christo Domino competit. Nemo certo inter nos, qui iura episcoporum laedere velit; sed cur non adhibentur verba, quibus omnis praetextus sinistrae institutionis sine ambagibus excludatur?")

26. *Mansi* 52, 1105 AB: "Apud omnes iurisconsultos aut iuris canonici doctores, apud omnia acta ecclesiastica dividitur potestas in ordinariam et delegatam. Omnes dicunt potestatem ordinariam, quae alicui competit ratione muneris, delegatam, quae non competit alicui ratione muneris, sed nomine alterius exercetur, in quo est ordinaria. Explicato sensu vocabulorum, lis ut videtur Deputationi, finita est."

100. This is what Vatican I taught. The term does not make the pope a first or a second ordinary of the dioceses, nor does it imply that papal authority is habitually exercised over the whole church.

101. Again before the voting began, Msgr. Zinelli spelled out in detail, what is to be understood by immediate: "Power which can be exercised without the necessity of having recourse to an intermediary is called immediate."[27] This is what Vatican I defined. The term *immediate* does not mean that papal authority is normally exerted over the whole church for daily issues, but it implies that the pope need not ask permission of a third party to exercise his primacy.

102. While leaving no one in doubt about the *extent* of papal jurisdiction ("over each and every one of the Churches, all the faithful and each individual") or about its *content* (*fides et mores*, discipline, church government), Msgr. Zinelli announced four limits before the vote.

- *First limit:* the same fullness of power resides also in the bishops, whether united in council or dispersed.[28] The definition does not imply that the bishop's power derives from that of the pope,[29] and changes nothing in the statute of the ecumenical council.[30]
- *Second limit:* papal jurisdiction is limited by natural law and by divine

27. *Mansi* 52, 1105 B: "Immediata est ea potestas, quae exerceri potest sine adhibito medio necessario, scilicet medio ad quod adhibendum tenemur."

28. *Mansi* 52, 1110 A: "We consider that the full and supreme power resides in the Sovereign Pontiff as head, and that the same utterly full and supreme power resides in the head united to its members, i.e. in the Pontiff together with the bishops." — "E contra nos admittimus vere plenam et supremam potestatem existere in summo pontifice veluti capite, et eandem vere plenam et supremam potestatem esse etiam in capite cum membris coniuncto, scilicet in pontifice cum episcopis . . ."

29. *Mansi* 52, 1314 A: "The definition according to which the entire plenitude of supreme power resides in the Sovereign Pontiff does not affect in any way the free discussion in the Schools of theories concerning the origin of Episcopal jurisdiction." — "Nullo modo per definitionem qua asseritur, totam plenitudinem potestatis supremae esse in summo pontifice, laeduntur sententiae, quae libere in scholis disputantur de derivatione iurisdictionis episcopalis. Disputant theologi, num potestas iurisdictionis, quae est in episcopis, derivetur immediate a Deo an immediate a summo pontifice."

30. *Mansi* 52, 1201 D: "In attributing full jurisdiction to the sovereign pontiff, it is in no way to be feared that this results in any kind of reduction of the status (dignitatem) of the ecumenical council." — "De plenitudine potestatis iurisdictionis in pontifice, in toto suo ambitu acceptanda, nulli ambigendi igitur locus; nec ulli scrupulum moveat quasi totam plenitudinem potestatis iurisdictionis tribuentes summo pontifici, ullo modo laedamus dignitatem concilii oecumenici."

law,[31] and normally also by the canons in force and by customary law.[32] According to divine law, the pope must respect Revelation and the previous council definitions, together with the church's constitution that includes the episcopate, and hence the need to respect the life of the dioceses, together with the forms of conciliarity and collegiality. Zinelli makes clear also that the pope cannot abolish the statute of patriarchs.[33]

- *Third limit*: the official explanation of the terms *ordinary, immediate, and truly episcopal* — the last one, however, not being part of the definition — gives the certainty that papal power is exercised only in cases of emergency.
- *Fourth limit*: Msgr. Zinelli again makes clear that papal power can only be exercised for "the edification of the church and not for its destruction." Destruction would be acknowledged if the pope put in peril the divine law, especially that of the episcopate.[34]

31. *Mansi* 52, 1108 D–1109 A: "This power is full in the sense that it can be limited *(coarctari)* by no supposedly superior human power; only by natural and divine law." — "Nam ex omnibus his fontibus revelationis apparet, Petro et eius successoribus datam fuisse veram plenam eamque supremam in ecclesia potestatem, scilicet plenam ita ut coarctari non possit ab ulla potestate humana ipsa superiore, sed a iure tantum naturali et divino". In the sentence immediately prior to this section these *fontes* are mentioned: sacra scriptura, traditio, definitiones conciliorum.

32. *Mansi* 52, 1109 A: "All moral theology proclaims that the legislator cannot overturn the wise and holy canonical arrangements deriving from the Church's apostles because he is himself bound by the same laws, which carry directive, yet not coercive force." — "Hinc vani et futiles . . . illi clamores, qui difficillime ut serii considerari possunt, ne si papae tribuatur perplena et suprema potetas, ipse possit destruere episcopatum, qui iure divino est in ecclesia, possit omnes canonicas sanctiones sapienter et sancte ab apostolis et ecclesia emanatas susque deque evertere, quasi omnis theologia moralis non clamitet legislatorem ipsum subiici quoad vim directivam, non quoad coactivam, suis legibus, quasi praecepta evidenter iniusta, nulla et damnosa possent inducere obligationem, nisi ad scandalum vitandum."

33. *Mansi* 52, 1103 BC: "Auctor 12ae emendationis eam etiam ob causam expungi vellet secundam hanc paragraphum, quia per verba 'cuiuscumque ritus et dignitatis' timet, ne videamur derogare privilegiis et iuribus patriarcharum orientalium. At consideret reverendissimus pater quod iam diximus, nos hic versari in privilegiis iure divino concessis Romano pontifice; ac proinde nos loqui de superioritate iure divino pertinente ad primatum; nullo modo igitur derogatur per definitiones, quae hic ferentur, privilegiis iure humano ac proinde mutabili forsan competentibus patriarchis."

34. *Mansi* 52, 1114 D: "No right-minded person could say that either the pope or an ecumenical council could destroy the episcopacy and the other realities of divine law." — "Et nemo sanus dicere potest, aut papam aut concilium oecumenicum posse destruere episcopatum caeteraque iure divina in ecclesia determinata." This is repeated similarly in 1116 A: "Nam quis

103. Also the concept of a *truly episcopal power* could be very ambiguous. Bishop de Las Cases of Constantine was suspicious; according to him, this choice had only one aim, i.e., "[t]o make the pope the one true bishop, with an immediate and ordinary function in every diocese, making the other bishops, though still bishops in name, in reality, mere vicars."[35] If — according to Zinelli — in the text preceding the canon, the jurisdiction of the pope was described as "truly episcopal," one has to understand by this that the jurisdiction of the pope has the same finality as that of a bishop, i.e., to feed the flock. But the expression — not having been taken up in the canon — is not part of the Catholic faith. Thus Vatican I does not teach that the pope is a bishop for the other bishops nor the bishop of the Catholic Church.[36]

104. Shortly after the suspension of Vatican I, the constitution *Pastor aeternus* was drawn into the German *Kulturkampf* by the Prussian Reichs-Chancellor Otto von Bismarck through the so-called *Circular-Depesche*,[37] written on May 14, 1872 but not published until December 29, 1874. Bismarck describes the relationship between the German Reich and the Holy See as subjected to intolerable stress by the Roman centralism and papal totalitarianism practiced by the Council.[38] This frontal attack from political quarters

---

suspicari posset, pontifici auctoritatem datam esse ad destructionem et non potius ad aedificationem ecclesiae?"

35. *Mansi* 52, 338: "Porro nihil aliud intendere videtur schema, nisi ut inducat novam pontificis iurisdictionem; quae adeo episcopos et dioceses singulas immediate et ordinarie involvit, ut solus revera maneat papa omnis ecclesiae episcopus, caeteri vero episcopi quoad nomen, vicarii quoad rem."

36. The title "Bishop of the Catholic Church," following the name of Paul VI subscribing the Acts of Vatican II, was used by the popes of the fourth and fifth centuries in their local synods to distinguish themselves from the other (rival) bishops of the same city. This title means *belonging* to the Catholic Church and not *over* the Catholic Church. See the philological study by Hilaire Marot, "Note sur l'expression 'Episcopus catholicae ecclesiae,'" *Irénikon* 37 (1964): 221-26. Georg May, *Ego N.N. Catholicae Ecclesiae Episcopus: Entstehung, Entwicklung und Bedeutung einer Unterschriftsformel im Hinblick auf den Universalepiskopat des Papstes.* Kanonistische Studien und Texte 43 (Berlin: Duncker & Humblot, 1995), tried to demonstrate such a universal episcopacy, mainly from medieval writings; he has been criticized in a review by Harald Zimmermann, *Zeitschrift der Savigny-Stiftung für Rechtsgeschichte, Kanonistische Abteilung* 84 (1998): 629-32.

37. In detail the Circular-Depesche complained that according to Vatican I the pope can usurp episcopal rights in every diocese and suspend the power of the local bishop. The episcopal jurisdiction is absorbed through papal power, and the pope can in principle replace any bishop, thus reducing the bishops to mere instruments in the hands of the pope and stripping them of any personal responsibility.

38. See *DH* 3112-17.

48

was refuted by the German episcopacy in a declaration that was signed by all bishops in the first months of 1875 as "definitely in opposition to the definitions" of the Council. Pius IX, in an *Apostolic Letter (Mirabilis illa constantia)* of March 4, 1875, then confirmed the interpretations of the Council given by the German bishops.[39] Pius IX went on to approve the measures taken by the German bishops "with the fulness of his Apostolic authority."[40]

105. Having examined what was in fact voted on at the Council, it becomes obvious, to sum up, that Vatican I did not make the pope an absolute monarch of the church.

2. Completing and Rebalancing Vatican I

106. A triple structural conditioning affects the pronouncements of Vatican I, by reason of its unintended interruption, its conceptual horizon, and its historical background.

- Because of the unintended and premature interruption of the Council, due to the Franco-Prussian War, only one of the schema's initially scheduled fifteen chapters could be discussed and adopted, i.e., that concerning the primacy, whereas nothing was said about the bishops as such. Such a truncated sequence of topics resulted in a *necessarily deficient statement* on the primacy. *It needs to be completed and balanced* by an adequate exposition of the Catholic faith concerning the church.
- However, the conciliar definition was not incomplete only by reason of historical contingencies. Another reason must be added: the structure of the Dogmatic Constitution *is deliberately centered on the papal office in*

39. Pius IX elucidates: "Die Klarheit und Gediegenheit Eurer Erklärung ist fürwahr so, daß sie, da sie nichts zu wünschen übrig läßt, nur Anlaß zu Unseren großartigsten Glückwünschen geben dürfte, wenn nicht die verschlagene Stimme bestimmter Zeitungen ein noch gewichtigeres Zeugnis von Uns erforderte, die, um die Kraft des von Euch zurückgewiesenen Schreibens wiederherzustellen, versuchte, Eurer Ausarbeitung die Glaubwürdigkeit abzusprechen, indem sie einredete, die Lehre der Konzilsdefinitionen sei von Euch gemildert und deswegen keineswegs entsprechend der Absicht dieses Apostolischen Stuhles gebilligt worden. Wir verwerfen deshalb diese durchtriebene und verleumderische Unterstellung und Andeutung; denn Eure Erklärung gibt die echt katholische und deswegen des heiligen Konzils und dieses Heiligen Stuhles Auffassung mit schlagenden und unwiderlegbaren Beweisgründen aufs geschickteste gestützt und glänzend erläutert . . . wieder . . ." (*DH* 3117).

40. Text published by Olivier Rousseau, "La vraie valeur de l'épiscopat dans l'Eglise," *Irénikon* 29 (1956): 150.

itself. A majority of the bishops saw in a reinforced papacy a protection for the freedom of the church and more generally a force for unity in the face of the modern world. The loss of the States of the Church in Italy (September 20, 1870) after the end of the Council (July 18, 1870) made the definition of the Council for the majority of bishops more convincing. The bishops were in fact traumatized by the Enlightenment and the French Revolution, by the progress of rational science, by the absolutism of modern states, by Gallicanism, and by episcopalianism and Febronianism. Hence, the collegiality of the bishops, the synodality of the ecumenical councils, the communion of the churches and their legitimate diversity, and the accountability of the pope, all these themes lost priority, leading to a serious systemic deficiency.

- Vatican I took place before historic consciousness had seeped into the minds of the bishops. For example, before the biblical renewal, the dispensing of power to Peter by Jesus appeared very differently from how it may appear today. The reception of Vatican I suffered from the same lack of sense for historicity: the canonical and disciplinary interpretations of the Council were seen in a sort of supratemporal light, fading out their timebound limitations.

107. To sum up: an analysis of the conceptual, systemic, and historical limits of Vatican I suffices to explain why Vatican II felt the need to integrate Vatican I into a comprehensive ecclesiological context. The question now is if it has sufficiently succeeded in this task.

3. Vatican I at Vatican II

108. Vatican II defines the dioceses as *portions* of the church, because they realize its essence. The Council's Decree on the Pastoral Office of Bishops in the Church, *Christus Dominus,* explicitly teaches it (CD 11):

> A diocese is a section [*portio*] of God's people entrusted to a bishop to be guided by him . . . so that . . . it constitutes one particular church in which the one, holy, catholic, and apostolic church of Christ is truly present and active.[41]

---

41. "Dioecesis est Populi Dei portio, quae Episcopo . . . pascenda concreditur, ita ut . . . Ecclesiam particularem constituat, in qua vere inest et operatur Una Sancta Catholica et Apostolica Christi Ecclesia."

109. The dioceses are not then parts of the church in the sense that all the parts, only when taken together, make up the complete being of the church. A diocese, without being the whole church, is nonetheless fully the church. This is the basis of eucharistic ecclesiology, a position more and more commonly shared between Catholics and Orthodox, which at the same time makes the singular *communion of the church* into a plural *communion of churches*.

110. Each diocese being a portion of the church, LG 23 teaches that "it is in and from these [particular churches] that the one and unique catholic church exists."[42] This essential statement completes and restores Vatican I to balance: since the church is seen as a communion of churches, the way is reopened, in principle, for dialogue between the churches. The *communio ecclesiae* is structured as a *communio ecclesiarum*.

111. Differing from Pius XII, Vatican II taught that bishops receive their mandate to govern directly from Christ.[43] A brief explanation is in order here. In the church, ordination is the basis of exercised authority. This applies equally to priests and bishops. In the consecration of a bishop, certain powers bestowed in principle already by presbyteral ordination are activated.[44] Vatican II removes the traditional canonical separation between sacramental power (which is conveyed by Christ in ordination and activated in the episcopal consecration) and pastoral charge or jurisdiction (which the bishop would receive from the pope, as Pius XII held). The bishop receives both the sacramental and the pastoral powers directly from Christ through ordination and episcopal consecration. Hence, we are to regard the bishops as "vicarii et legati Christi . . . neque vicarii Romanorum pontificum" ("vicars and legates of Christ . . . not . . . vicars of the Roman pontiffs" [LG 27]). According to the new CIC (1983), the authority of the bishops is no longer *derived* from the authority of the pope; the pope *reserves* to himself, for the sake of the unity of the universal church, certain prerogatives, which the bishops could also rightly exercise.

---

42. ". . . in quibus et ex quibus una et unica Ecclesia catholica exsistit."

43. *LG* 27: "Haec potestas qua nomine Christi personaliter funguntur, est propria, ordinaria et immediata . . ." ("This power, which they exercise personally in the name of Christ, is proper, ordinary and immediate . . .").

44. In regard to the relation between priest and bishop, see Hubert Müller, *Zum Verhältnis zwischen Episkopat und Presbyterat im Zweiten Vatikanischen Konzil: Eine rechtstheologische Untersuchung* (Vienna: Herder, 1971), and Hans Jorissen, "Behindert die Amtsfrage die Einheit der Kirchen? Katholisches Plädoyer für die Anerkennung der reformatorischen Ämter," in *Eucharistische Gastfreundschaft: Ein Plädoyer evangelischer und katholischer Theologen*, ed. Johannes Brosseder and Hans-Georg Link (Neukirchen-Vluyn: Neukirchener Verlag, 2003), pp. 85-97.

Henceforth, the bishop is responsible for his local church in the name of Jesus Christ and not in the name of the pope. Together with the other bishops he forms the college of bishops. The obligatory bishops' conferences (or the association of two or more bishops' conferences [CD 38.5]) might play a role analogous to that of the patriarchates of the ancient church (LG 23). The bishops' conferences could become a new framework for the churches to live in the communion of the church.

C. A Lutheran Response to the Interpretations of *Pastor Aeternus*

112. Lutherans are convinced that faith understood as trust is connected with the knowledge of what one is believing in. It can be expressed in sentences, in whom or in what one believes. This is the reason why in Martin Luther the "assertions" — statements that claim binding authority — play such an important role: "Tolle assertiones et Christianismum tulisti."[45] The point of the incarnation of God in Jesus Christ and the revealing activity of the Holy Spirit is not a skeptical reservation over against the binding character of all doctrinal statements — as was the case with Erasmus, according to Luther — but the certainty that God in his self-revealing allows himself to be recognized and definitively confessed. In his *Bekenntnis* that is added to his treatise *Vom Abendmahl Christi* (1528), Luther states: "I desire with this treatise to confess my faith before God and the whole world, point by point. I am determined to abide by it until my death and (so help me God!) in this faith to depart from this world and to appear before the judgment seat of the Lord Jesus Christ."[46] Insofar as the doctrine of infallibility aims to emphasize definite and wholly reliable statements of faith in the church, Lutherans will certainly be open for discussion.

113. Lutherans add, however, that any doctrinal statement that claims binding authority in the church must be based on Holy Scripture and that this reference to Scripture also be transparent. In that respect Lutherans operate with a *precise condition* for speaking of binding authority. To be sure, they are also aware that one cannot place Scripture and ecclesial doctrine on the same

---

45. *De servo arbitrio*, 1525, in *WA* 18, (551-99) 600-787, here 603, 28f.

46. Martin Luther, *Works* (Saint Louis: Concordia, 1955ff.), vol. 37, p. 360; *Vom Abendmahl Christi: Bekenntnis*, 1528, in *WA* 26, 261-509, here 499: ". . . so will ich . . . vor Gott und aller Welt meinen Glauben Stück für Stück bekennen, darauf ich gedenke zu bleiben bis in den Tod, darin — des mir Gott helfe — von dieser Welt zu scheiden und vor unseres Herrn Jesu Christi Richtstuhl kommen."

plane or play one off against the other or simply compare each with the other as if they were of the same literary genus. Rather one is bringing Scripture, *as it has opened itself up to certain Christians,* into relationship with a certain doctrine. This doctrine, in turn, claims to be direct or indirect interpretation of Scripture. The relationship, then, is not between Scripture itself and ecclesial doctrine, but Scripture as it is perceived and understood by certain people and ecclesial doctrinal statements, i.e., in the final analysis between different interpretations of Scripture that claim to advance the true meaning of Scripture.

114. That a possibly rather subjective and arbitrary interpretation of Holy Scripture by individual Christians could become the standard of judgment regarding ecclesial doctrinal statements, is a worry and concern of the Catholic teaching ministry that Lutherans can also share. However, they are no less worried and concerned about whether the pope overcomes this subjectivism regarding the interpretation of Holy Scripture, or whether he might not be its most striking instance, when he — as it appears to many — makes doctrinal decisions on his own authority. This is one way to formulate the Lutheran objection.

115. In regard to these worries and concerns, it is very important to note how in the two previous sections the doctrine of papal infallibility and the primacy of universal jurisdiction have been interpreted.

116. The interpretations developed above distinguish rightly and clearly between jurisdiction and infallibility. They argue from what the relevant commissions stated in the very debates of the Council itself concerning the interpretation of the decisions they were about to make. The explanations given partly reflect hesitations of bishops belonging to the minority at Vatican I, which are not unlike the Lutheran objections to the doctrine. The precise delineations of the competences of the pope, so plausibly expounded in both studies (A. and B.), are very important for the ecumenical dialogue. Furthermore, they refer to the fact that the Council was restricted in several respects. It was interrupted by the Franco-German war and, therefore, unable to treat the issue of authority in the church in a comprehensive way. The issue of the bishops in the church, their tasks and rights, was not debated in detail and formulated as ecclesial doctrine until Vatican II. The hermeneutical rule that the results of Vatican I must be read in the light of the statements of Vatican II is in line with these historical facts. In this way the content of what was accomplished in 1870 is preserved while at the same time seen in a more complex context. It is the presumption of the given interpretations that the one-sidedness of Vatican I, which resulted from the historical circumstances, in this way could be overcome.

117. The interpretations discuss another limitation that is due to the circumstances caused by movements such as Gallicanism and other threatening changes. The church felt harassed by powerful opponents and driven into a corner. In this situation it appeared to many bishops to be appropriate to place themselves in closed ranks under the strengthened authority of the pope. *Pastor aeternus* is understood by many Catholic theologians as a response to this situation and made plausible against that background. However, these past circumstances have long since ceased to prevail, and the Roman Catholic Church actually finds herself in a totally different situation. Times have changed, whereas the doctrinal response to the past remains, and irreversibly at that. The historical explanation promotes the historical understanding of the doctrine, but hinders, *e contra,* the systematic approach. Even though the above interpretations have shown that the pope in judgments that claim infallibility, as well as in the exercise of his jurisdiction, is bound and committed in many ways — bound to Scripture, tradition, and natural law, and committed to the *communio* of bishops — this is still not formulated explicitly and above all as precondition for the legitimacy of his decisions. If it were, the question would immediately be raised: *Quis judicabit,* i.e., by those who could argue that these preconditions have not been observed. The primacy of the pope would be relativized and be set in relation to another authority through submission to synodical structures, which would act as a counterbalance, if such a judging authority were in fact available. Confronted with the circumstances of the time, this is not what Vatican I actually wanted. What remains is the confidence and the firm expectation that the pope will act and decide as he should, objectively, although no one can enter such a plea canonically. Lutherans remain doubtful that Vatican II has quite overcome the one-sidedness of Vatican I.

118. It may be understandable that Christians from other churches do not easily muster the above-mentioned confidence in the discharge of the papal office. They have been living for centuries at a distrustful distance from the pope. Attitudes, feelings, theological judgments, which have developed during centuries, can only be changed in a long process of confidence-building measures and thus possibly be overcome. Changes necessary for such a process would have to be quite deep on both sides. If the Roman Catholic teaching authority wants to exercise its ministry so as to cause Christians and churches from outside the Roman Catholic Church to assent in faith to papal decisions, will its processes then not have to include the ecclesial doctrines and traditions of those other Christians in forming its judgments? Would non-Roman churches, in turn, not have to be open to contributing to a common truth-

finding process, and finally be prepared to recognize such a truth as binding?

119. It is important to maintain that the primacy of universal jurisdiction does not imply that the pope constantly interferes with the concerns of the dioceses, but does so only in emergencies. To be sure, the pope decides whether a given case constitutes an emergency or not. Once again, the confidence that the pope makes the right decision is at stake, and Christians from churches that are not recognized as churches in the proper sense of the term will have difficulties bringing such confidence to bear. On the other side, these Christians and churches will have to reflect whether there are not in fact problems of church order that could possibly be solved universally and in common. They will also have to consider whether refusing this universality — this "catholicity" — would not mean impairing their status as church.

120. The above-mentioned interpretations of the dogma of infallibility and the doctrine of universal papal jurisdiction open new avenues and possibilities for the ecumenical dialogue. They allow one to advance toward the core of the controversy instead of being occupied with issues that are finally secondary. The new interpretations represent a challenge for both sides, which becomes obvious by the simple fact that they are controversial in the Roman Catholic Church. Still, the Lutherans are convinced that they are the best and most appropriate interpretations of *Pastor aeternus* available. Even though — as is well known — the better interpretation of authoritative texts does not always prevail historically, it is still possible to count on the noncoercive power of the better argument.

D. Primacy of Doctrine and Jurisdiction — Necessary?
An Ecumenical Reflection

121. Since the Middle Ages and also in the Reformation period the popes and the papal theologians claimed that the ministry of the pope is a ministry *iure divino*. But at that time — considered dogmatically — this claim was only a claim; it did not belong to the official doctrines of the church. Vatican Council I in *Pastor aeternus* created a new situation. It has dogmatized the papal ministry as a ministry *iure divino*. This dogmatization makes it much more difficult for non–Roman Catholic Christians to develop a positive affinity with the primacy of the pope. Now the exegesis of *Pastor aeternus* and our discussions *ad rem* have shown that the Lutheran objections lodged at the time of the Reformation against the claim of *ius divinum* have been, in essence, taken into account. A

more precise and better-founded discussion on the powers of the pope as set forth in 1870 is now possible. What has not yet been treated is the question of the *necessity* for the church of the papal primacy of magisterium and jurisdiction.

122. First, it is important to note that the question of the *necessity* of primacy is no longer a question of its *salvific* necessity as it was in the time of the reformers. On the Catholic side, the papal ministry is no longer seen as necessary for salvation.[47] If that were not the case, the teaching of justification and hence the gospel and its primacy would, according to Lutheran thinking, be already placed in question here. Today the question as to the necessity of primacy is addressed to its *ecclesial* necessity, and hence to the question whether primacy is necessary for the *full* reality of the church.

123. This transformation of the question is of great importance, although it has to be said that for Lutheran thinking the question of the necessity of primacy also in its revised form — ecclesial, not salvific necessity — still remains problematic. For in the first place the *ecclesial* necessity of primacy also remains at least open to an interpretation in the sense of a *salvific* necessity and must clearly be separated or delimited from such an interpretation.[48] In the second place, and more especially, the question of the ecclesial necessity of primacy can in no case be answered in a way that would place in question or diminish the full ecclesial authenticity of the Lutheran churches, either in the past or in the present.

124. Here another differentiation could turn out to be crucial: namely, the difference between what is necessary *for the very being of the church* and what is necessary *for the unity of the church*. Admittedly, such a differentiation between the *being* and *unity* of the church also raises difficulties, since unity belongs to the essential attributes of the church: it belongs to its very being.[49]

---

47. To be sure, there are statements in the First Vatican Council that could still be understood in the sense of the *salvific necessity* of primacy (*ND* 822, 826, 837; *DH* 3056, 3060, 3071), even if they lack the categorical directness of the pronouncements of someone like Boniface VIII (his Bull *Unam Sanctam,* 1302) or Leo X (5th Lateran Council, 1516).

48. Here we should refer to the reflections and elucidations — in large part running parallel to the question of primacy — of the international Catholic/Lutheran dialogue in relation to the "ecclesial necessity" of the episcopal ministry in the apostolic succession: *Church and Justification: Understanding the Church in the Light of the Doctrine of Justification* (Lutheran World Federation, 1994); *Kirche und Rechtfertigung: Das Verständnis der Kirche im Licht der Rechtfertigungslehre* (Paderborn: Bonifatius Verlag, Frankfurt am Main: Verlag Otto Lembeck, 1994), pp. 97-102, no. 191-204.

49. We may think for example of the critical Observations on the Final Report of the International Anglican/Roman Catholic Commission (ARCIC) published by the Congregation

Yet the new openness to a form of primacy that is evinced in ecumenism today almost obliges us to make such a differentiation. For what is affirmed as important in primacy in non-Catholic Christianity, and what is expected of it, is quite clearly its service to the *unity* of the universal church, not the help it would give to the other churches to achieve the fullness of their being as church. But that means: the whole of the non-Catholic expectation of primacy is premised on just this distinction between *church* and *unity of the church,* and is aimed at the latter. The new ecumenical openness to primacy will stand or fall on the success or otherwise of this differentiation. It would be lost once again if this differentiation did not take hold and primacy had to be understood strictly and without any differentiation as "necessary for the very being of the church." It follows that in the shared discussion of the question of primacy, this differentiation between "church" and "unity of the church" should emphatically be borne in mind and should not be regarded from the outset as a road we cannot go down.[50]

125. The above interpretations of *Pastor aeternus* have opened a door for ecumenical understanding in regard to another issue: the Reformation insistence on the ability to critique decisions of the papal magisterium as based on the gospel. Given that the teaching of Vatican I did not exclude but rather implied that the pope is subject to the superior norm of the gospel, then this implication smoothes the path to a Catholic-Lutheran accord on the issue of infallibility. Here too, as in the case of the primacy of jurisdiction, along with assiduous attention to discerning the content of Holy Scripture, an alert ecumenical sensibility is required in assuming the ministry of care for the *communio ecclesiarum,* for the unity of the churches.

---

for the Doctrine of the Faith (March 27, 1982): "According to Catholic tradition, visible unity is not something extrinsic added to the particular churches, which already would possess and realize in themselves the full essence of the Church; this unity pertains to the intimate structure of faith, permeating all its elements. For this reason the office of conserving, fostering and expressing this unity in accord with the Lord's will is a constitutive part of the very nature of the Church" (*AAS* 74 [1982] 1062-74, quotation 1070).

50. That this path is not closed is shown by the relation of the Catholic Church to the Orthodox Churches of Eastern Europe, whose rejection of the papal primacy of jurisdiction does not — in the Catholic judgment — place in question their claims to be a church, though it does preclude her full ecclesial unity or communion with these churches.

Confessional Approaches to the *communio ecclesiarum* and the Service of Unity

A. *Communio ecclesiarum* and the Service of Unity in the Lutheran Churches

126. Lutheran churches have received their particular character in their striving to restore the continuity with the church of the apostles and with the apostolic gospel, which according to the judgment of the reformers the church of their time had lost or had obscured. Since in the sixteenth century the question of far-reaching religious reforms, as triggered by the preaching and teaching of the reformers, continued to belong also to the sphere of responsibilities of the leading political authorities (emperor, princes, magistrates), such reforms were impossible without these authorities. So their involvement was immediately enlisted, whether it be to promote or to suppress the reforms. There were territories in which those reforms were possible, and others in which they were impossible: in some territories the Lutheran Church could be established and develop, while in others it could not. That goes not only for Germany, but also for Scandinavia. In the Peace of Augsburg of 1555 the followers of the Augsburg Confession were officially granted religious freedom within the domains of the Holy Roman Empire, but this right was only given to rulers and not to their subjects, according to the policy of *cuius regio, eius religio.* In the Peace of Westphalia (1648) religious freedom was extended more widely to the Reformed churches. As a result of these historical circumstances the Lutheran churches have a strong territorial characterization. Since the bishops in the German Empire were at the same time princes, the office of bishop in the traditional sense was not preserved in the Lutheran churches in Germany, in

contrast to the situation in Scandinavia. Lutheran communities and churches then arose in many other countries as a result of emigration and mission.

127. Lutheran churches have always made the claim to catholicity, even when this claim conflicted with their territoriality. At the end of the first part of the *Augsburg Confession* (CA) it is forcibly underlined (in Art. XXI):

> Haec [Art. I-XXI] fere summa est doctrina apud nos, in qua cerni potest nihil inesse, quod discrepet a scripturis vel ab ecclesia catholica vel ab ecclesia Romana, quatenus ex scriptoribus nobis nota est.[1]

128. The ordination testimonials of the ordinations practiced in Wittenberg since 1535 refer with particular emphasis "always to the doctrinal correspondence between 'ecclesia nostra' and the 'catholica ecclesia Christi'; Luther (in connection with the Apostles' Creed) understood the latter to mean the 'whole Christian Church.' Added emphasis was given to this in the testimonials since 1542: 'uno spiritu atque una voce cum ecclesia catholica Christi.' . . . In the same way reference is made to the accusation of the 'fanaticae opiniones' through the 'iudicium catholicae ecclesiae Christi.' . . . The fact that since the summer of 1542 . . . explicit reference is always made to the need 'iuxta doctrinam apostolicam' (see especially Ti 1:5 and Eph 4:8 and 11) for teaching office and the administration of the sacraments to be transferred to the ordinand through public ordination can be interpreted in the same sense."[2] Just as with the catholicity of their churches, the Lutheran churches also maintain their continuity with the early church. Luther declared that "we abide by the true early church, indeed we are the true early church."[3] In his letter to Duke Albrecht of Prussia in 1532, Luther lays emphasis on the fact that "the article on the Last Supper has been peaceably believed and held firm throughout the world from the very beginning of the Christian church right down to the present hour, as is shown by the books and writings of the dear Fathers, both in Greek and Latin. . . . For it is dangerous and dreadful to hear or to believe something that runs counter to the concordant witness, faith and doctrine of

---

1. "This is nearly a complete summary of the teaching among us. As can be seen, there is nothing here that departs from the Scriptures or the catholic church, or from the Roman church, insofar as we can tell from its writers." *The Book of Concord: The Confessions of the Evangelical Lutheran Church* (Minneapolis: Fortress Press, 2000), p. 59. See also here (58) the (longer) version of the text, originally in German.

2. *WA Br.* 12, 448 (introduction of the editor to the ordination testimonials).

3. *Wider Hans Worst*, 1541, in *WA* 51, (461-68) 469-572, here 479, 17: "wir bey der rechten alten Kirch blieben, ja . . . wir die rechte alte Kirche sind."

the holy Christian church as a whole, in the way it has been peaceably adhered to from the beginning to the present day for over fifteen hundred years."[4]

129. Luther can also speak quite impartially of the apostolic succession:

> The Apostles . . . were called directly by Christ himself, just as the prophets in the Old Testament were called by God. The Apostles later called their disciples, as Paul did Timothy, Titus, etc. They in turn then called bishops, as Tit 1 says, while the bishops have called their successors right down to the present time and so on to the end of the world.[5]

1. Communio ecclesiarum — *Inner-Lutheran Communion*

130. The Lutheran churches are autonomous churches. Yet they share in common what is most important: they profess the Holy Scriptures of the Old and New Testament to be the only source and norm of their doctrine, life, and service. They see in the three Ecumenical Creeds and in the Lutheran Confessions, especially in the unaltered *Augsburg Confession* (CA) and the *Small Catechism* of Martin Luther, a valid exposition of the Word of God.[6] That is the doctrinal foundation of the Lutheran World Federation (article II of its Constitution). This goes for all the Lutheran churches. That not all these churches are members of the Lutheran World Federation depends on the circumstance that some of them are of the opinion that, in spite of sharing the same confession in content, their understanding of it differs.

131. According to CA VII, "agreement concerning the doctrine of the Gospel and the administration of the Sacraments" *(consentire de doctrina evangelii et de administratione sacramentorum)* is necessary and sufficient for the unity of the church. In the 1950s Lutheran theologians developed a particular con-

---

4. In *WA* 30/III, (541-46) 547-53, here 552, 5-15.

5. "Est itaque divina vocatio duplex, una mediata, altera immediata. Deus vocat nos hodie omnes ad ministerium verbi vocatione mediata, hoc est vocatione quae fit per medium, id est, per hominem. Apostoli vero immediate vocati sunt ab ipso Christo, sicut prophetae in veteri Testamento ab ipso Deo. Apostoli postea vocaverunt suos discipulos, ut Paulus Timotheum, Titum etc. Qui deinde Episcopos, ut Tit. 1., Episcopi suos successores vocaverunt usque ad nostra tempora et deinceps usque ad finem mundi, Et haec est vocatio mediata, quia per hominem fit, et tamen divina est": *In epistolam S. Pauli ad Galatas Commentarius ex praelectione D. Martini Lutheri collectus,* [1531] 1535, in *WA* 40/I, 59, 16-23.

6. Recognition of the doctrinal decisions of the first four ecumenical councils as correct exposition of the Holy Scripture is implicitly affirmed therein (more explicitly than in the Formula of Concord).

cept of church communion, in order to determine in theological and practical terms the relation of Lutheran churches to each other and also the relation between the churches created through the Reformations of the sixteenth century. In the theses of the plenary assembly of the Lutheran World Federation in Minneapolis (1957) we thus read:

> For our Lutheran Churches with their diverse history and in their different situations and challenges of the present time, what is meant by "it is sufficient" (in CA VII) is the overcoming of barriers of a local, national and organizational kind, and demands of us the expression of our unity at the table of the Lord, where we share in the one Body.[7]

132. Where an agreement in the understanding of the gospel and in the celebration of the sacraments exists, church communion, understood as pulpit and altar fellowship, can and should be declared. Since the ordained ministry serves the communication of the gospel and the celebration of the sacraments, the recognition of that communion in the preaching of the gospel and administration of the sacraments means that the ministry itself is implicitly recognized. This reciprocal recognition of ministry and ordination in the participating churches now occurs also expressly with the declaration of church communion. What this reciprocal recognition intends, is, where possible, joint action of the churches ("witness and service") and a joint clarification of what the gospel means in contemporary situations, as well as what follows from it or is bound up with it or is even excluded by it. At the LWF plenary assembly in Budapest in 1984 Article III, 1 of the Constitution was revisited: since then it affirms that "all member churches understand themselves to be in pulpit and altar fellowship." The plenary assembly in Curitiba in 1990 declared that the LWF is "a communion of churches."

133. In such a *communio ecclesiarum,* the question arises of its depth or intensity. It is not enough, after all, just to have a common Confession. The Confession, like Holy Scripture, whose binding interpretation the Confession claims to be, constantly needs to be newly understood, newly interpreted, and adapted to new situations in new contexts — both in a diachronic and synchronic sense. Given this need for a continuing interpretation of Scripture and Confession and the recurring task of the churches to take decisions on life in

7. Thesis II, 5, cited after Peter Brunner, "Der Lutherische Weltbund als ekklesiologisches Problem," in Peter Brunner, *Pro Ecclesia: Gesammelte Aufsätze zur dogmatischen Theologie,* vol. 2 (Berlin and Hamburg: Lutherisches Verlagshaus 1966), pp. 232-52, here 247.

the church and in the world, it is also needful to preserve and gain a shared doctrine of the gospel as the basis for the *communio ecclesiarum.* This in turn grounds the need to sustain the awareness of, and the means to reach, common statements on doctrine and common decisions, so that the declaration of the *communio* of the churches corresponds to an actual communion in the teaching, proclamation, and life of the churches.

134. If the *consentire de doctrina evangelii et de administratione sacramentorum* (CA VII) permits the *communio* of the Lutheran churches, the same *communio* should also exist in the enactment of that doctrine, at any rate in the sense of a mutual duty of accountability and regular joint consultations on questions of doctrine. If the service of doctrine in this sense is exercised in a wider context than that of the individual churches, this will help to relativize particular problems and perspectives and also help to take seriously the insights of other churches. The Lutheran World Federation has repeatedly undertaken this task and, on behalf of the Lutheran churches, reached a common position also on questions of doctrine. An example of this is the Resolution of the LWF plenary assembly in Budapest (1984) suspending the membership of the white churches in South Africa that had not ended the division of their churches on racial grounds and had not unambiguously condemned the apartheid system. A further example is the Joint Declaration on the Doctrine of Justification that was signed in Augsburg in 1999 by the representatives of the LWF and the Roman Catholic Church after an extensive consultation and decision-making process in the Synods of the Lutheran Churches and in the LWF itself. The worldwide Lutheran community thus definitely has at its disposal the means to issue common statements on doctrinal questions.

135. Of course, both these examples also show that significant reservations and oppositions exist in the individual churches to binding doctrinal statements and church-governing functions that transcend the autonomous local churches. The process of common decision-making is shown in practice to be very difficult. All too often one can point to shortcomings in the catholicity and the binding nature of decisions that are signed not only by the local churches but also at the supra-regional level.

2. Communio ecclesiarum *Worldwide*

136. This worldwide *communio* cannot be enough for the Lutheran churches, neither in its intensity nor in its extension. As far as its extension is concerned, there are very many people who through their baptism in the triune God

belong to the body of Christ and profess faith in this God and his salvation in the one church, but who nonetheless belong to churches with which the Lutheran churches are not in communion. That is a contradiction that needs to be addressed, if the Lutheran churches and Christians are to take seriously the confession of belonging to the one, holy, catholic, and apostolic church, as enunciated in the third article of faith. So the ecumenical opening and mission of the Lutheran churches follows from their faith in the Holy Spirit. In this task the first thing to be done is to examine what other churches, that claim to be Christian churches, teach on the gospel and how they administer the sacraments, and also — since the gospel does not preach itself and the sacraments are not self-administered — how they envisage the participation of the faithful in the communication of the gospel and how they realize this (ministry and priesthood of all the baptized). The task posed here is to recognize things held in common that permit another communion to be recognized as Christian, in other words, as an apostolic church. The second task is to examine what are the obstacles that stand in the way of a reciprocal recognition of communions as Christian churches, how great these obstacles may be, and how they can be overcome.

137. The above-described understanding of church communion in the Lutheran churches is based on CA VII. Yet, though for the *Augsburg Confession* the *consentire de doctrina evangelii et de administratione sacramentorum* is expressed in the articles of the Confession itself, the concept of church communion described in it has also been addressed by non-Lutheran Evangelical churches. Thus the *Leuenberg Agreement (Leuenberger Konkordie)* of the *Fellowship of Reformation churches in Europe* was already signed in 1973. Under this Agreement "churches with different confessional positions" ("Kirchen verschiedenen Bekenntnisstandes") declared themselves to form a church fellowship among themselves, several years before the LWF assemblies in Budapest and Curitiba. In the *Leuenberg Agreement* the understanding of unity enunciated in CA VII was thus adopted in modified form. It is not, as it is in the fellowship of Lutheran churches, *an explicit common confession* that lies at the basis of the communion of churches; rather, church communion is explained in the link with the confessions that exist in the participating churches, with an appeal to *a common understanding of the gospel* which is, in its content, outlined in the Agreement. The Agreement thus has the role of a bridge: it expresses that the triune God and his redemptive action in the world are professed in the different confessions. In this way a differentiated consensus is reached: a consensus that differentiates between content and expression in language and concept, between center and periphery, between perennial and

more timebound forms of thought, and so on. On the basis of CA VII the question of ministry is further explicitly addressed in the *Leuenberg Agreement,* as in the concept of church communion described above. The question of ministry is unavoidable in any joint statement on church communion, since the recognition of the true teaching of the gospel and the right administration of the sacraments means the *de facto* recognition of the ministry, and any declaration on church communion implies *ipso facto* certain statements on ministry: church communion can only be explained if there are institutions in the participating churches that are in the position to declare church communion for these churches. Insofar as a certain degree of doctrinal agreement is a necessary prerequisite for the declaration of church communion (and that must be so if a communion can fulfill the claim to be an apostolic church), then there must be in addition a doctrine that is binding in these churches, as well as some kind of *episkopē* to guarantee that such doctrine will also be enacted in the proclamation of the Word and the administration of the sacraments. When church communion with separated churches is declared in connection with CA VII, this article from its own inner impulse leads on beyond itself.

138. As a result of the ecumenical work of the Lutheran churches, a series of declarations of church communion have been issued, beginning at the regional level. Alongside the above-mentioned Leuenberg church fellowship (1973; now the Community of Evangelical Churches in Europe), we may cite the *Meissen Agreement* between the Church of England, the Union of the Evangelical Churches in the German Democratic Republic, and the Evangelical Church in the Federal Republic of Germany (1988); the *Porvoo Common Statement* between the British and Irish Anglican churches and the Nordic and Baltic Lutheran churches (1992); the *Reuilly Common Statement* between the Anglican churches of Great Britain and Ireland and the Lutheran and Reformed churches of France (1999); and *Called to Common Mission* between the Episcopalian Church and the Evangelical-Lutheran Church in America (1999/2000).

139. With the *Joint Declaration on the Doctrine of Justification* (1999) the Lutheran World Federation and the Roman Catholic Church declared that "a consensus in basic truths of the doctrine of justification exists between Lutherans and Catholics" (No. 40; GiA II, 573). And: "The teaching of the Lutheran churches presented in this declaration does not fall under the condemnations from the Council of Trent. The condemnations in the Lutheran confessions do not apply to the teaching of the Roman Catholic Church presented in this declaration" (No. 41; GiA II, 573). Given the fact that differences

could not yet be removed in the same way on the question of the sacraments and especially of the ministry, the Joint Declaration did not yet lead to a *communio ecclesiarum* of the Lutheran churches with the Roman Catholic Church. In the understanding of what should be meant by the visible unity of the churches, important differences persist between the Catholic Church and Lutheran churches: they concern the value to be attached to the *communio episcoporum* and especially the office of the pope.

B. *Communio ecclesiarum* and Service to Unity in the Roman Catholic Church

140. In his above-mentioned encyclical *Ut unum sint,* Pope John Paul II invited the leaders of the non–Roman Catholic churches and their theologians to engage with him "in a patient and fraternal dialogue." This leads directly to a related question: What can Roman Catholic theology, for its part, contribute so that such a dialogue, a dialogue namely with the other Christian churches on a universal ministry of church unity, can bear fruit?

1. *Ecclesiological Guidelines of the Second Vatican Council*

141. The following remarks cannot pretend to present any comprehensive ecclesiology of the Second Vatican Council. Yet some points of view may be emphasized that would be worth developing in ecumenical dialogue with a view to the restoration of the *koinonia* of the churches. The First Vatican Council had already taken up the question of church. Corresponding to the post-tridentine controversial theology and the neo-scholasticism of the nineteenth century, the schema presented to this Council was dominated by an understanding of the church that essentially considered what the church is from the perspective of official church ministry. Hence Vatican I developed no comprehensive view of the church and limited itself, or had to limit itself, to the definition of the universal papal primacy of jurisdiction and the infallibility of the pope. Between the First and Second Vatican Council, and especially after the First World War, a lively ecclesiological debate began; the theological understanding of the church and its renewal was reviewed, in connection with the youth movement, the liturgical movement Ament, and the ecumenical movement that was only then emerging in the Roman Catholic Church. Romano Guardini, Karl Adam, Manes Dominikus Koster, the abbeys of Beuron and Maria Laach,

the theologians of the Nouvelle Théologie (such as Yves Congar, Marie-Dominique Chenu, Henri de Lubac), Karl Rahner, and Heinrich Fries all played their part in this theological discussion. A theological enrichment of the ecclesiology of the Catholic Church by these and other theologians would not have been possible, however, without *ressourcement,* pondering the theological understanding of the church in the Fathers of the Church, as in John Henry Newman and in the theologians of the Catholic Tübingen school of the first third of the nineteenth century, despite all their limitations; nor without an encounter, however timid, with contemporary Protestant theology.

142. The many-sided efforts to deepen our understanding of the church and to renew it bore ample fruit in the Second Vatican Council (SC, LG, UR, GS), even if a minority fought strenuously for the maintenance of a neo-scholastic understanding of the church and was also able to incorporate its prerogatives into important passages of the Council's texts. The result is that many Vatican II texts on crucial questions bear the signs of a compromise that is not always free of contradictions. Nevertheless, these were not able to obscure some basic intentions of church renewal. In the two fundamental theological opening chapters of LG, "The Mystery of the Church" and "The People of God," the communion of all the baptized, the general or, in the words of the Council, the "common priesthood" of all the faithful, is addressed, and discussed again in chapter IV of LG ("The Laity"). The designation of the People of God is linked with the choosing of Israel. It is not the church but Jesus Christ, however, who is the "light of the nations." "The church, in Christ, is a sacrament — a sign and instrument, that is, of communion with God and of the unity of the entire human race" (LG 1). This church of Jesus Christ subsists in the Roman Catholic Church (LG 8); this does not exclude that many elements of sanctification and truth can also be found outside its structure, and since these are gifts belonging to the church of Christ, they are forces impelling towards catholic unity. With reference to LG 8, spelled out more fully in UR 3 and 4, the encyclical *Ut unum sint* stresses (Nos. 13 and 14), "It is not that beyond the boundaries of the Catholic community there is an ecclesial vacuum." "Many elements of great value *(eximia),* which in the Catholic Church are part of the fullness of the means of salvation and of the gifts of grace which make up the church, are also found in the other Christian Communities" (No. 13). "Ecumenism is directed . . . to making the partial communion existing between Christians grow towards full communion in truth and charity" (No. 14).

143. At the present time a lively Roman Catholic debate has developed about what should more precisely be understood by the *subsistit* of LG 8: Can it be understood as an ecclesiological clause that is inclusive and outward-

looking in intention and that favors ecumenism, as most conciliar fathers and Roman Catholic theology have understood it after the Council, and as it has also been shown to advantage in the ecumenical dialogue of the churches? Or should it be interpreted, instead, as the confirmation of the ecclesiological exclusivity claim of the Roman Catholic Church as handed down since the Council of Trent? It is also unclear in LG 8 how the "catholic unity" should be understood, toward which "many elements of sanctification and of truth" that are found outside of the structure of the Roman Catholic Church are impelling. Repeated Roman declarations not to pursue any "return-to-the-fold" ecumenism, but to search, in common with the other churches and church communities in the one ecumenical movement, for the unity of the church that Jesus Christ wants for his church, can appeal to Vatican II's Decree on Ecumenism that gives concrete expression to LG 8.

144. In UR 3 it is underlined that the Holy Spirit has not refrained from using the other Christian churches as *media salutis*. This points to the understanding of the *subsistit* of LG 8 as furnishing an ecclesiological opening. In LG 15 the sacramental union of all the baptized and the many features that all Christians have in common are underlined, including the sacraments that they "recognize and accept in their own churches or ecclesiastical communities" (LG 15). Chapter III of LG, devoted to the hierarchical structure of the church, is the one most influenced by the understanding of church passed on from the First Vatican Council. And yet it underlines the theological significance of the office of bishop and the collegiality of the bishops in contrast to the one-sided emphasis on the office of the pope bequeathed by that council. It thus recognizes the bishops' synods as an important function for the government of the church. In this sense the universal church is understood as *communio ecclesiarum*. The only dogmatic correction of a decision of the Council of Trent follows in LG 28: Trent spoke of a divinely instituted hierarchy that consists of bishops, priests, and deacons (ND 1708 and 1719; cf. DH 1765 and 1776), whereas Vatican II speaks of divine institution only in relation to "the divinely instituted ecclesiastical ministry" as such, which is then "exercised in different degrees [or "orders"] by those who even from ancient times have been called bishops, priests and deacons" (LG 28). An outstanding chapter of LG is the one on the laity (IV) (general priesthood, participation in the redemptive mission of the church, eligibility to hold offices that serve spiritual goals, etc.). Never before in her history had the Roman Catholic Church expressed herself so fundamentally and in such a theologically comprehensive way. Of great ecumenical significance is, lastly, the profession of faith in a church "at once holy and always in need of

purification," a church that "follows constantly the path of penance and renewal" (LG 8; cf. UR 6).

145. In spite of numerous perspectives for the renewal and reform of the church, Vatican II was unable to develop a uniform ecclesiology. Within a single text it juxtaposed two ecclesiologies that cannot be brought into harmony. We find them placed side by side, unconnected, in LG: on the one hand, the ecclesiology of *communio* of the early church, which acknowledges a theologically founded and canonically structured collegiality of the bishops, as well as a real *communio ecclesiarum,* without the subordination of all churches to one church in particular; and, on the other, a Roman centralist ecclesiology that defines itself starting from the papacy. This has led in the reception process of Vatican II to a series of Vatican pronouncements and theological debates on problems that have to this day led to no satisfactory conclusion. The most important aspects of this debate are: the significance of Bishops' Conferences, the relation between local church and universal church, the relation of the church of Jesus Christ to the Roman Catholic Church *(subsistit)* and the understanding of church as *communio.* These problems, discussed with great vehemence, and the Vatican pronouncements on them, have also given rise to ecumenical debates. Central problems here involve chiefly the tropes of fullness/completeness versus shortcomings, of concentric circles of Christian churches revolving round the Roman Catholic Church, and ultimately a self-understanding of the Roman Catholic Church that sees, in any ecclesial form other than her own, a church with inherent defects, one that cannot be recognized as a church in the true sense. The problems mentioned make it clear that the Council was not the conclusion of the renewal and reform of the church, but only the beginning of their beginning.

2. The Role of Doctrine in Canonical Norms

146. Vatican II intended to reform the structures of the church. As regards the further considerations, it is necessary to distinguish between the doctrine of the church on the one hand and canonical norms that are to implement, promote, and protect the doctrine through actions on the other hand. It is also necessary to differentiate between the norms and the application of the norms. The teaching and the acting church must be distinguished, but not separated: they are intrinsically linked.

147. The CIC following Vatican II is to some extent a novum in the Roman Catholic Church. Until then canonical norms mostly found their source in

customs or in responses to specific disputed issues of earlier periods. Since over the course of time many norms from different sources (e.g., councils, popes, bishops, synods, customs) were in force, it became unclear which norms had superseded others and which laws would now be valid. Gratian's *Concordia Discordantium Canonum,* also known as *Decretum Gratianum* (ca. 1140), is an example of clarifying these difficulties; however, it was never officially promulgated. Vatican I asked for a collected, simplified, newly organized system of laws. The format chosen for it relates to the self-understanding of the Catholic Church as *societas perfecta.* In analogy to many Western nations a Codex was fashioned and in 1917 it was promulgated by the pope himself. It was structured according to the law books of the Roman jurists Gaius and Justinian and a textbook on canon law published in 1563 by John Paul Lancelotti. The norms reveal a certain ecclesiology, but they were as a whole not conceived on a specific ecclesiology. Nevertheless a subsequent interpretation of the norms might be governed by a certain theology, which in fact took place when the maximalist interpretation of the doctrine of Vatican I became the guiding understanding of the norms on primacy in the 1917 Codex.

148. Quite different in its format is the 1983 Code of Canon Law: in promulgating this new Codex, Pope John Paul II said that the doctrinal insights of Vatican II had to be "translated" into canonical norms;[8] according to him these teachings should determine both the structure of the norms and the content. Because canonical norms have the purpose of assisting the community to live and act in agreement with its belief, these norms in relation to doctrine have repercussions for understanding the process of drafting, interpreting, and applying the law. When drafting a norm, the legislator decides first which doctrinal aspects are in need of support by way of canonical norms in order for the doctrine to shape the life of the community. Subsequently, the legislator searches for a fitting modality that will allow the community to act in accordance with the doctrine and thus "receive" the doctrine.

149. For several reasons it is important to differentiate between these two steps of identifying the doctrine and determining a fitting modality.

---

8. "Immo, certo quodam modo, novus hic Codex concipi potest veluti magnus nisus transferendi in sermonem canonisticum hanc ipsam doctrinam, ecclesiologiam scilicet conciliarem. Quod si fieri nequit, ut imago Ecclesiae per doctrinam Concilii descripta perfecte in linguam canonisticam convertatur, nihilominus ad hanc ipsam imaginem semper Codex est referendus tamquam ad primarium exemplum, cuius lineamenta is in se, quantum fieri potest, suapte natura exprimere debet." John Paul II, "Apostolic Constitution 'Sacrae disciplinae leges,'" in *AAS* 75 (1983): p. xi; English translation: *Code of Canon Law,* Latin-English Edition, New English Translation (Washington, DC: Canon Law Society of America, 1998), p. xxx.

- *First,* this distinction between the doctrine and the modality makes it possible to evaluate the identification of the doctrine by the legislator as well as the modality chosen. Did the legislator receive the doctrine fully or only partially? If only certain aspects were received and others not, what must be done to remedy this situation? Did he choose a modality fitting for this specific community here and now?
- *Second,* the distinction between doctrine and modality will allow for a better response in case of a nonreception of the norm by the faithful. Does the reason for the nonreception lie with the doctrine or with the modality? In case the doctrine governing the norms is not received by the community, the response must occur on the level of the teaching office. In case the modality is not (any longer) fitting for the community for which the norm is issued, another modality must be sought. Then canonists must respond.[9]
- *Third,* the differentiation allows for plurality and diversity in unity: the modality might change either over the course of history, because different accents of the doctrine need to be emphasized at different times[10] or because the situation and means available have changed in such a way that a different modality is necessary. It may also be that there are different modalities from one community to another simultaneously, because the needs, means, and circumstances differ from one community to another.[11]

150. In interpreting and even more so in applying canonical norms, that is, when law and life meet, it is necessary once more that the doctrine deter-

---

9. The canonical institution of *ius remonstrandi* implies that a diocesan bishop indicates to a higher legislator that a certain law cannot be binding for his diocese, because it is not agreeable to or fitting for his community. The communication has a suspending effect: the law is not binding for the community.

10. The sacrament of reconciliation is a good example. Its modality did not only change over the course of history, but the sacrament was also referred to by different names to emphasize one or other aspect of its doctrine more intensely at a specific point in time, such as reconciliation, forgiveness, penance, confession.

11. An excellent example can be found in the constitutions of religious institutes, which differ due to their different spiritualities. Canon Law determines, for example, that a community *(domus)* must have a superior, but it is left to the constitutions to determine whether the superior is elected, presented, or appointed. Canon law determines that the superior must have a council, but it is for the constitutions based on the spirituality of the institute to determine whether the council has mainly an advisory role to the decisions made by the superior or if the council together with the superior decides on virtually all issues.

mines the hermeneutical perspective for reading both the norms and the situation in which the norms are to be applied. Thus, for example, care must be taken that the situation to which the law is to be applied is formulated in the perspective and language of the conciliar doctrine, which has to govern the belief of the church. The norms may not be considered in isolation from the whole doctrine. Three dangers must be avoided.

- *First,* the maximalist interpretation must not be used to interpret the law. Even if in drafting the norms a maximalist interpretation would have been influential, that does not imply that a subsequent maximalist interpretation is permitted as well. Only by taking into consideration the whole doctrine does an awareness of the bearing of a particular doctrinal aspect emerge. This in turn provides insight into the reasons for any omissions and insertions.
- *Second,* a positivistic interpretation by which the norms are detached from the doctrine itself would be incorrect and wrong.
- *Third,* a presumption according to which the norms themselves would directly reveal the binding doctrine for the community would also be misleading, since it "upgrades" the norms themselves to the status of doctrines; this contradicts the differing character and purpose of both doctrine and law.[12]

12. When only a certain part of the doctrine is received in the canonical norms and subsequently these norms are seen as the only binding doctrine, then the canonical norms are given a doctrinal authority that does not do justice to the nature of canonical norms: doctrine belongs to the teaching church, canonical norms to the acting church. Moreover, such an understanding would not allow for an evaluation of the norms in light of the doctrine and would risk an immutable canonical system, because there would not be any doctrinal criterion on the basis of which the canonical norms should be changed. An example: Vatican II stated that the bishop is *vicarius Christi* (*LG* 27) for the diocese entrusted to his care. This is a doctrinal expression. There is no need to repeat it in canonical norms. It is however necessary to ask what this expression means for the juridical competencies of a diocesan bishop. The doctrine leads to the norm that a diocesan bishop "in the diocese entrusted to him has all ordinary, proper, and immediate power which is required for the exercise of his pastoral function" (c. 381). Then is added how this is to be seen in relation to others who might hold power as well. The canon adds: "except for cases which the law or a decree of the Supreme Pontiff reserves to the supreme authority or to another ecclesiastical authority." In case there is a doubt about the competency of a diocesan bishop, recourse must be taken to the doctrine that he is the vicar of Christ and that thus it must be presumed that he can act as long as the matter has not been reserved to someone else. To argue that the bishop is not the vicar of Christ, because the canons would not say so, but "a civil servant of the pope," stands in total contradiction to the doctrine expressed in both Vatican I and Vatican II that must govern these norms. Of

151. In practice, in order to determine the doctrine with regard to the Petrine ministry one has to consult the documents of Vatican I as well as of Vatican II. The Constitution on the Church of Vatican Council II, *Lumen gentium,* repeats sections of Vatican I and adds new insights. Both old and new elements here appear side by side without mediation in the form of juxtapositions. For determining the present-day doctrine, Vatican II has to be used as a kind of lens to read Vatican I. Yet, the juxtapositions of Vatican II complicate the challenge of a faithful determination of the doctrine of Vatican II. This is not an easy task.

152. Pope John Paul II was well aware of this and spoke about old and new elements in the Council as he promulgated the 1983 Code of Canon Law. He stated that the newness of the Council had to determine the newness of the Code.[13] With regard to the ecclesiology of Vatican II he said that the newness consisted in particular in "the doctrine in which the Church is presented as the People of God (cf. LG, chapter II), and authority as a service (cf. LG, chapter III); the doctrine in which the church is seen as a 'communion,' and which, therefore, determines the relations which should exist between the particular churches and the universal church, and between collegiality and the primacy; the doctrine, moreover, according to which all the members of the People of God, in the way suited to each of them, participate in the threefold office of Christ: priestly, prophetic and kingly . . . and finally, the Church's commitment to ecumenism."[14]

153. This statement has two implications that are intrinsically connected: *First,* they urge that the doctrine on the Petrine ministry must govern the drafting, interpretation, and application of canonical norms in light of the doctrine on the *communio ecclesiarum.* The one doctrine cannot be seen without the other. This will have repercussions for the *second* aspect, namely the restoration of the unity of the church.

154. Pope John Paul II urges explicitly that the commitment to Christian unity is to be a decisive factor in the actions and being of the church.[15] This

---

course doctrine must be the criterion again to determine whether that which is reserved to others is indeed theologically correct, for example, because the unity of the church would require it.

13. See also Myriam Wijlens, "'The Newness of the Council Constitutes the Newness of the Code' (John Paul II): The Role of Vatican II in the Application of the Law," in *Proceedings of the Canon Law Society of America* (Washington, DC: CLSA, 2008), pp. 285-302.

14. John Paul II, *Sacrae disciplinae leges,* p. xxx (see above, note 8).

15. On the occasion of the twenty-fifth anniversary of the promulgation of the Code of Canon Law, Cardinal Walter Kasper gave a lecture on January 11, 2008. He addressed in par-

commitment is qualified as "irreversible" by the pope in his encyclical *Ut unum sint*[16] and is to permeate the whole church also in its actions. It implies that every modality in canon law must also face the question: Is it ecumenically conducive or not? If not, it will be necessary to search for another modality.[17] On the level of the interpretation and application of the law, the commitment implies that the unity of the church must be a governing factor as well: Does the application of the law in this specific case further, or hamper, the unity?

155. When the two aspects, namely understanding the doctrine on Petrine ministry in light of the *communio ecclesiarum* and the commitment to the restoration of Christian unity are seen together with regard to canonical norms, then doors are opening up to ecumenism. Given the distinction between doctrine and modality,[18] not only should the doctrine govern the form of the exercise of the Petrine ministry, but the commitment to the restoration of unity must also constitute a guiding principle of high priority in searching for a fitting modality.

156. A change in canonical structures will be inevitable, but it should be noted that there is no need to await such a change; in fact an acting that is in agreement with the whole doctrine of Vatican II, which implies a correct reading of Vatican I, is not prohibited by the current law. Nor is it forbidden "to

---

ticular the commitment to the restoration of Christian unity and its hermeneutical implications for canon law. An English translation has been published as "Canon Law and Ecumenism," in *The Jurist* 69 (2009): 171-89.

16. John Paul II, "Encyclical letter 'Ut unum sint,'" *AAS* 87 (1995): 921-82, English translation: *Encyclical Letter Ut unum sint of the Holy Father John Paul II on Commitment to Ecumenism* (Washington, DC: United States Catholic Conference, 1995); also *Ut unum sint: Encyclical Letter of the Holy Father John Paul II on Commitment to Ecumenism* (London: Catholic Truth Society, 1995), no. 3.

17. The "Peter and Paul Seminar," an international research group of theologians and canon lawyers, attend to the question, which canonical institutions can and must be modified in order for the Catholic Church to be more conducive to Christian unity. The Seminar is inspired by the Groupe des Dombes' publication *Pour la conversion des églises: Identité et changement dans la dynamique de communion* (Paris: Centurion, 1991), English translation *For the Conversion of the Churches* (Geneva: WCC, 1993). See also Myriam Wijlens, "Peter and Paul Seminar: A Follow Up by Theologians and Canon Lawyers to the Groupe des Dombes' Publication 'For the Conversion of the Churches,'" in *Rethinking Ecumenism: Strategies for the 21st Century,* FS Anton Houtepen, ed. Freek L. Bakker et al. (Zoetermeer: Meinema, 2004), pp. 229-41; reprint in *The Jurist* 64 (2004): 6-20. In 2004 the Peter and Paul Seminar focused on collegiality of bishops, in 2007 on the bishop and the local church, and in 2009 on Conversion and Reform in the Church. The proceedings of the conferences are published in *The Jurist* (1999, 2004, 2008-9).

18. *UUS* 95.

listen to the voice of the particular churches."[19] This could indeed pave the road to a new modality as *ius sequitur vitam.*

Excursus: On the Authority and Binding Character of Roman Catholic Magisterial Texts and Curial Documents

157. Up to this point, the subject has been postconciliar church legislation: canon law in relation to the doctrine of the church. Before turning now to the authority of postconciliar documents of the Curia bearing on the understanding of church — pronouncements that have aroused considerable irritation among Catholics and in ecumenical circles — it may be in order to address in general the issue of the authority and binding character of Roman Catholic doctrinal statements. For every Christian church the Holy Scripture of the Old and New Testament has a binding character because it is both the fundament and the norm of the faith. For the Roman Catholic Church the dogmatic decisions of all councils also have a binding character, including the unilateral decisions of Western Roman Catholic councils after the separation of the churches in the eleventh and sixteenth centuries. In addition the papal infallible doctrinal definitions claim a binding character, e.g., the dogmatic definitions of 1854 and 1950. But even infallible definitions of the pope or of councils are surrounded by a fallible milieu. To this fallible milieu belong, to mention only a few:

- The question of the opportunity of a definition
- The pattern of ideas of a definition
- The interpretation of a definition
- A sinful dealing with the opponents of a definition
- The incomprehensibility of the language of a definition, which makes a reception of a definition by the people either more difficult or nearly impossible.

158. This fallible milieu does not participate in the infallibility of a definition, but is caught up with it, and it is difficult to separate one from the other.[20]

19. Congregatio pro Doctrina Fidei, "Il Primato del Successore di Pietro nel mistero della Chiesa," *Communicationes* 30 (1998): 205-16. English translation, *L'Osservatore Romano* (31 October 1998): 7.

20. See Karl Rahner, "Kirche und Parusie Christi," in Karl Rahner, *Schriften zur Theologie,* vol. 6 (Einsiedeln, Zürich, Cologne: Benziger Verlag, 1963), pp. 348-67, here 363. ET in Rahner, *Theological Investigations,* vol. 6 (New York: Crossroad, 1982).

For this reason even authoritative infallible doctrinal decisions can be corrected within the framework of their possibility of overall improvement.

159. Within the Roman Catholic Church also, non-infallible authentic official statements of the teaching office, whether of the pope, of his Curia, or of the pope together with the bishops, claim a binding character. Such authentic official statements are, e.g.:

- Papal encyclical letters
- Papal documents published as *Motu proprio*
- Apostolic constitutions
- Statements, letters, notifications, etc. of the Roman Curia, especially those of the Congregation for the Doctrine of the Faith, authorized by the pope to publish them.

160. The authority of these texts comes from the content as well as the degree of binding force accruing to them by reason of the category chosen for their publication.[21] One must avoid overrating or underrating these documents. The texts deal with very different and various problems, quite often with questions of doctrine, of interchurch and interreligious relations, moral or liturgical issues, and church discipline. Even when these texts pronounce a judgment on such questions and problems, they are, taken as a whole — by their nature and in dogmatic perspective — provisional. They are not exempt from discussion, to which they frequently lead within the church, even if they intend to end a discussion.

161. This is also the case with the documents from the Congregation for the Doctrine of the Faith since 1992 that have espoused positions regarding the understanding of church, furrowing many a brow. We will come back to them below in Chapter IV.B.1. In general, however, these statements have but a modest doctrinal weight; what they treat could also be changed again. Such revisions have occurred in the course of history repeatedly. To mention only two examples:

1. The Second Vatican Council contradicted important passages of the encyclical *Mystici corporis* (1943) and presented a more comprehensive view of church.
2. In its Declaration on Religious Liberty, the Second Vatican Council defends the "Right of the Person and Communities to Social and Civil Liberty in

---

21. For the categories of Roman Catholic documents, see Heiner Grote, *Was verlautbart Rom wie? Eine Dokumentenkunde für die Praxis* (Göttingen: Vandenhoeck & Ruprecht, 1995).

Religious Matters"[22] and thereby tacitly revokes the condemnation of religious liberty in the Syllabus of 1864.[23]

3. Primacy of Jurisdiction in Contemporary Roman Catholic Canon Law

162. Large parts of the church and many bishops and bishops' conferences throughout the world have welcomed the church reforms and ecumenical opening brought by Vatican Council II and are working on their further development. At the same time, however, the new Code of Canon Law of 1983, which itself is intended to be the conversion into canon law of the decisions of Vatican II, hardly developed the concepts of the collegiality of the bishops and those of a true *communio ecclesiarum.*

163. If one takes a purely positivist or a maximalist interpretation of the relative canons in regard to the powers of the pope, the risk is great of failing to do justice to the focus of Vatican II. For the most part, the canonical texts repeat those formulations in LG that are taken over from the First Vatican Council with its maximalistic rendering. The new Codex only partially incorporates the new aspects of Vatican II, however. According to the CIC, the Bishop of the Roman Church is the head of the College of Bishops *(Collegii Episcoporum caput),* the Vicar of Christ *(Vicarius Christi),* and the Pastor of the universal church here on earth *(universae Ecclesiae his in terris Pastor).* By virtue of his office, he has *supreme, full, immediate,* and *universal* ordinary power in the church, and can always freely exercise his power.[24] This power that is peculiar to him is exercised by the Pontifex Romanus not only *in* the church as a whole, but also *over* all the particular churches and their groupings; he enjoys ordinary and immediate power over them. He exercises his office in connection with the other bishops, but he can decide whether to exercise it personally or in the collegial context.[25] No appeal or recourse is permitted

22. Dignitatis humanae 1.

23. *ND* 1013/15; *DH* 2915.

24. Can. 331 — "The bishop of the Roman Church, in whom continues the office given by the Lord uniquely to Peter, the first of the Apostles, and to be transmitted to his successors, is the head of the college of bishops, the Vicar of Christ, and the pastor of the universal Church on earth. By virtue of his office he possesses supreme, full, immediate, and universal ordinary power in the Church, which he is always able to exercise freely."

25. Can. 333 — "§1. By virtue of his office, the Roman Pontiff not only possesses power over the universal Church but also obtains the primacy of ordinary power over all particular churches and groups of them. Moreover, this primacy strengthens and protects the proper,

against a sentence or decree of the Roman Pontiff.[26] In this connection it is determined: "The First See is judged by no one" (can. 1404), corresponding to the old principle of canon law: *Papa omnes iudicat, sed a nemine iudicatur.*

164. In the perspective of a purely maximalist interpretation the decisions of (Roman Catholic) ecumenical councils, Bishops' Synods, etc. only obtain legal force if they are enforced by the pope as the head of the College of Bishops, which cannot be active without its head, and as the supreme legislator, judge, and administrator. He possesses an episcopal authority in every single diocese, an authority that is concurrent with and superior to the authority of the diocesan bishop. The pope can take in hand things that he normally does not deal with and issue regulations that can neither be altered nor revoked by any subordinate authority. The maximalist interpretation through the CIC of texts of Vatican II, in which Vatican I is reiterated, implies that the power of the pope includes the supreme teaching power, including infallibility in *ex cathedra* decisions (and in conciliar decisions) in matters of faith and morals.

165. A purely positivist interpretation of the new Code of Canon Law sees in it the true interpretation of the teaching of Vatican II. This view runs counter however to the intentions of the popes John XXIII, Paul VI, and John Paul II, which regard the postconciliar legislation expressly as "translating" the conciliar teaching into canonical norms. Their perspective emphasizes that the teaching of the Council is to serve as a lens that one should use in framing the law but also in interpreting the canons. Even if significant statements of Vatican II did not find their way into the postconciliar lawgiving, nevertheless the conciliar teaching in its full extent is to be employed in the interpretation of the canonical texts. This is decisive for reflection about the future of the papal ministry. The entire teaching of the Second Vatican Council is the framework for the interpretation and application of the canonical provisions regarding the pope. The teaching of Vatican II on the collegiality of bishops, on the local church (which is church in the fullest sense, LG 26), on the *sensus fidelium,* and on the *communio ecclesiarum* serves the same purpose.

166. A further indication of the scant canonical reception of the ecclesi-

---

ordinary, and immediate power which bishops possess in the particular churches entrusted to their care." — "§2. In fulfilling the office of supreme pastor of the Church, the Roman Pontiff is always joined in communion with the other bishops and with the universal Church. He nevertheless has the right, according to the needs of the Church, to determine the manner, whether personal or collegial, of exercising this office."

26. Can. 333 — "§3. Contra sententiam vel decretum Romani Pontificis non datur appellatio nec recursus."

ology of Vatican II is how the relationship of universal and particular church is conceived in the CIC of 1983. There one finds little evidence of the dogmatic new orientation with a view to a *communio* of local churches in the structure of the church. Without any doctrinal mandate, the 1983 Codex imposed on canonical language the terminology *universal church/particular church (ecclesia particularis),* thus weakening the concept of communion of churches. The neologism "particular church" — unknown to the 1917 Codex — is supposed to describe the dioceses technically and exclusively.[27] This normative choice is debatable, for in the Latin languages and in English, and especially in German *(Teilkirche), particular* is, from the dictionary's viewpoint, the antonym of universal. Hence, the word choice seems to take for granted that churches termed "particular" are not rightful partners in the church universal; they are spontaneously understood as parts of, and no longer as churches in, the universal church.

167. From 1993 to 2007, a series of disciplinary documents from the Roman Curia[28] underlined once again the priority (and superiority) of the communion of the church over the communion of churches. These documents, of which *Communionis notio* (1992) is the prototype, build upon the binomial universal church/particular church of the 1983 Code to claim chronological and ontological priority of the universal church through its universal maternity:

> Indeed, according to the Fathers, *ontologically,* the Church . . . that is one and unique, precedes creation, and gives birth to the particular Churches as her daughters. She expresses herself in them; she is the mother and not the product of the particular Churches. . . . From the Church, which in its origins and its first manifestation is universal, have arisen the different local

27. In the Decree *Christus Dominus* concerning the pastoral charge of bishops, *ecclesia particularis* was introduced as the equivalent of the term diocese, which fifty-seven Fathers took rather as the designation of an administrative unit ("imperial in origin and administrative in nature," "originis imperialis et indolis administrativae," *Acta Synodalia Sacrosancti Concilii Oecumenici Vaticani II*, vol. 3, periodus tertia, pars VI [Vatican City: Typis Polyglottis Vaticanis, 1975], p. 162). Hence the Council decided that "dioecesis generatim diceretur 'Ecclesia particularis,' sed in titulo addi debet 'seu dioecesis,' ut significetur quaestionem esse de illis particularibus Ecclesiis, quae hodie dioeceses vocantur" (p. 163). In any case, the term *ecclesia particularis* was introduced without even mentioning the relation between the dioceses and the church as a whole. There are only twelve occurrences of the expression *ecclesia particularis,* whereas the term *diocese* is used ninety-one times, and a further fifty-one times in its adjectival form.

28. For a fuller discussion of the ecumenical problems of these documents, see Chapter IV.B.1.

Churches, as particular expressions of the one unique Church of Jesus Christ. Arising *within* and *out of* the universal Church, they have their ecclesiality in it and from it.[29]

168. Such a motherhood is unknown to tradition,[30] just as is the statement according to which "the ministry of the Successor of Peter, (is) not only (seen) as a 'global' service, reaching each particular Church from 'outside,' as it were, but as belonging already to the essence of each particular Church from 'within,'"[31] appearing to make of the Bishop of Rome a kind of universal bishop, an idea rejected by Pius IX after Vatican I.

169. The majority of the theologians expressed reticence[32] at this idea[33] — to say the least — rejoining that of Cardinal Kasper, who rightly feared seeing confusion between the maternity of the universal church and that of the Church of Rome, saying that the formulation risks becoming exceedingly problematic, if the one universal church is identified with the Church of Rome — in fact with the pope and the Curia. Should this be the case, then the letter of the Congregation for the Doctrine of the Faith cannot be understood as a help in clarifying the ecclesiology of communion, but has to be understood as its abandonment, and as an attempt at theological restoration of Roman centralism.[34]

170. In summary: half a century after Vatican II, the realization of the idea of the church's communion as a communion of churches still remains a distant prospect. In this period the status of the international bishops' synod claimed

29. "Communionis notio," *AAS* 85 (1993): 838-50, here no. 9.

30. The tradition does of course recognize a) that one church can be mother of another, as its founder; b) the motherhood of the heavenly Jerusalem; c) the holy church as mother in faith of all believers.

31. "Communionis notio" (see note 29), no. 13.

32. Of the thirty or more Catholic ecclesiologists who have addressed the subject in all languages, only one claims to be convinced, although without giving reasons; list drawn up by A. Cattaneo, "La priorità della Chiesa universale sulla Chiesa particolare," *Antonianum* 77 (2002): 503-39; with minor additions by Hervé Legrand, "La théologie des églises soeurs: Reflexions ecclésiologiques autour de la déclaration de Balamand," *RSPhTh* 88 (2004): 461-96, here 495-96.

33. In matters of faith, of course, there is a priority of the Church over the local churches. In these matters one church alone cannot decide of the true faith that is handed down precisely through a process of *traditio* and *receptio,* which holds the churches together in *communio.*

34. Walter Kasper, "Zur Theologie und Praxis des bischöflichen Amtes," in *Auf neue Art Kirche sein: Wirklichkeiten-Herausforderungen-Wandlungen,* FS Bischof Josef Homeyer, ed. Werner Schreer and Georg Steins (Munich: Bernward bei Don Bosco, 1999), pp. 32-48, here 44.

by Vatican II, of the national bishops' conferences,[35] of the diocesan synods,[36] or of the liturgical powers of the bishops,[37] has permanently been weakened.

171. Should we conclude from this that the influence of the *plenitudo potestatis* of Vatican I had really turned the Catholic bishop into a "papal functionary," as Max Weber anticipated?[38] And done so to such a fundamental extent that Vatican II was unable to halt this transformation, now accomplished in the 1983 Code, and in the disciplinary arrangements that followed?[39]

172. Does the dogma of the pope's full and universal jurisdiction inevitably lead to an ecumenical impasse? Such a conclusion would be ill-founded in Catholic *theology.* It would fail to take account of the weak doctrinal status of disciplinary statements, or of the fact that the prevailing law and its implementation can be dissociated from theology. And something else is evident, namely that for the best Catholic dogmaticians the rereading of the Vatican I dogma is a legitimate enterprise that is already well underway. The current *"relecture"* of the dogma of papal jurisdiction with the aid of a comprehensive hermeneutics of dogma is highly promising. It leads into a landscape that contrasts markedly with the prevailing discipline.

35. "Motu proprio 'Apostolos suos,'" *AAS* 90 (1998): 641-58, especially numbers 12, 13, 19, 21, which see these conferences as creations of the Holy See, and invite them above all to follow the magisterium of the universal church, acknowledging them to be authentically magisterial only on condition of unanimity.

36. "Instructio 'De synodis diocesanis agendis,'" *AAS* 89 (1997): 706-27, no. IV. 4, which obliges the bishops to ban discussing at a synod disciplinary matters that pertain only to an authority superior to that of the diocese.

37. "Instructio 'Liturgiam Authenticam,'" *AAS* 93 (2001): 685, no. 80: the Holy See retains strict control over liturgical translations into the vernacular, as "an exercise of the power of governance, which is absolutely necessary."

38. Commenting upon Vatican I, he wrote, "Und in der Kirche war nicht etwa das vielberedete Unfehlbarkeitsdogma, sondern der Universalepiskopat der prinzipiell wichtige Abschluß (des vatikanischen Konzils im Jahre) 1870. Er schuf die 'Kaplanokratie' und machte im Gegensatz zum Mittelalter den Bischof und Pfarrer zu einem einfachen Beamten der kurialen Zentralgewalt." Max Weber, *Wirtschaft und Gesellschaft: Grundriss der verstehenden Soziologie,* Studienausgabe, ed. Johannes Winckelmann, 5th rev. ed. (Tübingen: J. C. B. Mohr [Paul Siebeck], 1980), p. 825; see also Max Weber, *Gesammelte politische Schriften,* ed. Johannes Winckelmann, 2nd enlarged ed. (Tübingen: J. C. B. Mohr [Paul Siebeck], 1958), p. 309.

39. This is the diagnosis of the current situation by a canonist whose method is admittedly purely positivist: "Die allgemeinen kodikarischen Bestimmungen zum Episkopat und zum Diözesansbischofsamt sowie die normative Ausgestaltung dieses Amtes in den kodikarischen Bestimmungen zeichnen den Diözesanbischof rechtlich als päpstlichen Beamten." Georg Bier, *Die Rechtsstellung des Diözesanbischofs nach dem Codex Iuris Canonici von 1983,* Forschungen zur Kirchenrechtswissenschaft 32 (Würzburg: Echter Verlag, 2001), p. 376.

4. Theological Considerations

173. The attention just now given to canon law has pointed out the contrasts between the whole span of Vatican II teaching on ecclesiology and its downplaying through overemphases and omissions in canonical and administrative practice. The purpose has been to seek possibilities of a new approach toward opening an ecumenical conversation on the papacy.[40] If one also takes into consideration a theological critique that draws on the results of the historical study of theology and dogma and harvests the ecclesiology of Vatican II, a theological interpretation can point out ways to an ecumenical understanding of the papal ministry.

174. First, it should be recalled that the First Vatican Council wished to understand its decisions "according to the ancient and constant belief of the universal Church" (ND 818/3; DH 3052), in the way it "is also contained in the proceedings of the ecumenical Council and in the sacred Canons" (ND 825; DH 3059), especially those "in which the Western and Eastern churches were united in faith and love" (ND 831; DH 3065). Cardinal Ratzinger tried to do justice to the historical facts when he declared: "Nor is it possible . . . to regard as the only possible form and, consequently, as binding on all Christians the form this primacy has taken in the nineteenth and twentieth centuries." In this connection he emphasized at the same time "that what was possible for a thousand years is not impossible for Christians today," following this up with the observation: "Rome must not require more from the East with respect to the doctrine of primacy than had been formulated and experienced in the first millennium."[41] Even earlier Joseph Ratzinger had expressed himself in favor of a clear differentiation of the offices bound up with the Bishop of Rome: Bishop of Rome, Metropolitan of the Roman Ecclesiastical Province, Patriarch of the West, and Primate of all Bishops. He also pleaded for the establishment of new patriarchates wherever necessary, and for their autonomy from the Latin church.[42]

175. With regard both to the dogma of infallibility and that of the primacy of jurisdiction, it is well to note the following. The First Vatican Council saw

40. On the fundamental relation between Holy Scripture, dogmatic teaching tradition, and teaching office in the church, see in more detail Chapter IV.

41. Joseph Ratzinger, *Theologische Prinzipienlehre: Bausteine einer Fundamentaltheologie* (Munich: Wewel Verlag, 1982), p. 209. ET: *Principles of Catholic Theology* (San Francisco: Ignatius Press, 1987), p. 198.

42. Joseph Ratzinger, *Das neue Volk Gottes: Entwürfe zur Ekklesiologie,* 2nd ed. (Düsseldorf: Patmos Verlag, 1970), pp. 142-46.

the dogmas of papal *infallibility* as a provision in view of an emergency situation threatening the *fides* and the *mores*. With the dogma of the *primacy* of jurisdiction, as explained, the First Vatican Council did not wish to set aside the usual customs and ways of communication for discipline and teaching in the life of the church. These statements do not carry conviction unless the juridical primacy is invoked in exceptional circumstances only, in the case of an emergency situation involving the unity of the church in discipline and doctrine. It is at any rate clear that Vatican I did not lend its authority to any maximalist implementation of its decrees.

176. Therefore the current canon-law provisions can only in a very limited way appeal to the decisions of Vatican Council I and II. They are indebted — as mentioned above — to a maximalist interpretation of Vatican I as well as to the fact that the ecclesiological and theological debates at Vatican I mainly dealt as a rule with the problem of papal infallibility, not with the papal primacy of jurisdiction and its implications. The primacy dogma however deserves the same theological attention as infallibility. Primacy of jurisdiction and infallibility, although of different theological origins, hang very closely together in juridical perspective. On the juridical level papal infallibility is nothing but the supreme, full, immediate, and exclusive power on the level of teaching in the form of *ex cathedra* decisions in matters of faith and morals, related to revelation. A consequence of the primacy of jurisdiction at the level of teaching is also that the decisions of the church's teaching office need to be followed with religious obedience *(obsequium),* also in teachings that are not infallible. Though the Second Vatican Council enunciated other ecclesiological principles (People of God, ecclesiology of *communio*), it also allowed the ecclesiology of papal centralism to stand.

177. If the current canon-law provisions are to be altered in such a way as to foster a ministry of unity of the universal church that could be accepted by all churches, the first prerequisite would be for Roman Catholic theology to discuss the jurisdictional primacy of the pope in such a way as to place it in a position, with the aid of a newly thought-out dogmatic interpretation, freed from conventional canonical precedents, to reflect in an open fashion with the other churches on the need for, and the form of, a ministry of unity of the universal church in the *koinonia* of the churches.

178. The alteration of canon law, however, is only possible if its dogmatic basis in terms of its aptitude for change and improvement is examined beforehand and if the result of this examination produces a positive reply. The alteration of teaching in the sense of its improvement and deepening is dogmatically ever possible, if — as Thomas Aquinas taught — the necessary distinction

between *res* and *enuntiabile* is first made.[43] With regard to the primacy of jurisdiction, the definition itself and what it defines is the *enuntiabile,* but the act of faith is addressed not to it, but to what is intended by it, i.e., its meaning, at the *res* that is intended by it. The *sensus dogmatum,* the meaning of dogmas, according to Vatican I, is to be adhered to,[44] and this meaning — and this goes for all teachings — should, according to Vatican II, be increasingly deepened.[45]

179. If such a distinction is drawn, then the meaning of the infallibility dogma and the primacy of jurisdiction could be objectively established as follows:

- helping to ensure the unity of the church in fundamental questions of Christian faith in cases where it is threatened;
- ensuring the freedom of the proclamation of the gospel and the free nomination to ecclesial offices in all social systems.

180. The *absolutist form,* which has clothed this guarantee, is however not a content of the faith. By paying attention to such a distinction, Catholic theology would also be free, together with other churches, to reflect anew on how what is intended by the primacy of jurisdiction could best be ensured today. In the case of the primacy of jurisdiction it is possible in any event to hold firm to what is *intended* thereby, while giving it a wholly new form (e.g., conciliar, synodal, synodally confirmed, ecumenical, etc.), and at the same time to reject the primatial form that has been given to it since Vatican I, in the context of an absolutist papacy, and successively developed thereafter in canon law.[46] One

43. "Actus autem credentis non terminatur ad enuntiabile, sed ad rem," *Sth* II-II, 1, 2 ad 2. Thomas speaks of the object of the faith in the same *quaestio* in distinguishing between "ipsa res credita" and "enuntiabile," *Sth* II-II, 1, 2c.

44. *ND* 136; *DH* 3020.

45. E.g., *UR* 4: In ecumenical dialogue "each explains the teaching (doctrina) of their communion in greater depth (profundius) and brings out clearly its distinctive features. . . . [A]ll are led to examine their own faithfulness to Christ's will for the church and, wherever necessary, to undertake with vigor the task of renewal and reform."

46. On the collegial-synodal collaboration in the exercise of the primacy, a broad agreement of opinion is evident among respected theologians such as, e.g., Walter Kasper (see Ch. V, notes 5 and 6); the cardinals Martini and Danneels and the archbishop John R. Quinn have made similar proposals. Cf. Hermann Josef Pottmeyer, "Recent Discussions on Primacy in Relation to Vatican I," in *The Petrine Ministry: Catholics and Orthodox in Dialogue,* ed. Walter Kasper (New York: Newman Press, 2006), pp. 210-30; Hermann Josef Pottmeyer, *Towards a Papacy in Communion: Perspectives from Vatican Councils I and II,* trans. Matthew J. O'Connell

can adopt an analogous approach in relation to church office or authority, for the concept of "hierarchy" tends to stand in the way of, rather than to open access to, an appropriate theological understanding of church office and of *episkopē* as a necessary element of service in, not over, the church. Leaving behind the unbiblical usage of "hierarchy" could let the basis of the theological understanding of church office that is held in common be articulated more distinctly.[47]

181. These are just a few "indications for a viable way" to necessary reforms — in the sphere of definitive doctrine as well. Whether an agreement of the other churches is possible as to what is intended by primacy of jurisdiction, while at the same time letting go of its absolutist form, can only be tested and established in dialogue with them.

C. Appendix: Honorary Primacy in the Early Church and *communio ecclesiarum* — Brief Survey

182. This appendix makes no claim to completeness, nor is it a product of firsthand research. Rather it is merely a short comparative account of the role played by the theme of *communio ecclesiarum* in the Orthodox churches, in the churches of the Anglican Communion, and in the Methodist churches. It provides a succinct overview of how in each case *communio ecclesiarum* is seen

---

(New York: Crossroad, 1998); also by Pottmeyer: "Die zwiespältige Ekklesiologie des Zweiten Vatikanum: Ursache nachkonziliarer Konflikte," *Trierer Theologische Zeitschrift* 92 (1983): 272-83; "Kirche als Communio: Eine Reformidee aus unterschiedlichen Perspektiven," *Stimmen der Zeit* 210 (1992): 579-89; "Kontinuität und Innovation in der Ekklesiologie des II. Vatikanums," in *Kirche im Wandel: Eine kritische Zwischenbilanz nach dem II. Vatikanum,* ed. Giuseppe Alberigo, Yves Congar, and Hermann Josef Pottmeyer (Düsseldorf: Patmos Verlag, 1982), pp. 89-110; Johannes Brosseder, "Visionen eines 'Petrusdienstes' im 3. Jahrtausend: Zum theologischen und ekklesiologischen Horizont eines Amtes universalkirchlicher Einheit," in *Der Dienst des Petrus in der Kirche: Orthodoxe und reformatorische Anfragen an die katholische Theologie,* ed. Johannes Brosseder and Wilm Sanders (Frankfurt am Main: Verlag Otto Lembeck, 2002), pp. 103-24, here 111-21.

47. Medard Kehl makes the case for doing without the concept of hierarchy, arguing that the subjection of the community under a sacred authority is anti-scriptural, since it is in conflict with the fundamental equality of all the faithful: Medard Kehl, *Die Kirche: Eine katholische Ekklesiologie* (Würzburg: Echter Verlag, 1992), p. 115; further Bernd Jochen Hilberath, "Communio hierarchica: Historischer Kompromiß oder hölzernes Eisen?," *Theologische Quartalschrift* 177 (1997): 202-19, here 211-18; *Paul Hoffmann,* "Der 'Stiftungswille Jesu': Das hierarchische Amtsverständnis der römischen Kirche im Spiegel des Neuen Testaments," *Orientierung* 70, no. 13/14 (2006): 154-60 (Lit.).

and experienced. It is evidence that the subject of the present study, even apart from the Lutheran-Catholic dialogue, is a much-discussed topic. In addition, the patristic idea and reality of a primacy of honor is first noted, without going into it in any detail.

1. The Honorary Primacy in the Early Church

183. In the early church the designation and practice of honorary primacy, or the preeminence of particular churches, played an important role. At the Council of Constantinople (381) it was determined in Canon 3 that the Bishop of Constantinople had an honorary primacy (presbeia tès timès, *honoris primatus*),[48] second only to that of the Bishop of Rome, by virtue of the fact that the city of Constantinople was younger than the city of Rome. In Canon 28 of the Council of Chalcedon (451) the primacy of the Church of Constantinople as second in primacy to the Church of Rome was reaffirmed, again with the

48. According to the councils of Constantinople and Chalcedon the primacy of honor of the churches of Rome and Constantinople is based on the political function of both cities as capitals of the Roman Empire. But for the life of the church the following viewpoint became more important: "In the patristic era, the churches considered to have been founded by apostles *(sedes apostolicae)* had normative roles in clarifying the content of true faith in Christ. But from the second century onward, the Church of Rome, where Peter and Paul were venerated as martyrs, claimed to be 'apostolic' in a singular manner" (*The Apostolicity of the Church: Study Document of the Lutheran–Roman Catholic Commission on Unity*, ed. Lutheran World Federation and the Pontifical Council for Promoting Christian Unity [Minneapolis: Lutheran University Press, 2006], 47, no. 86). In Late Antiquity bishops, presbyters, synods from both the West and the East, repeatedly appealed to Rome requesting an intervention in situations of conflict. They sought support for their positions and hoped to obtain from Rome a decisive solution (47, no. 86). This shows the high reputation of the Church of Rome; it belongs to the context of the primacy of honor and cannot be taken as evidence for the recognition of the primacy of jurisdiction of the Church of Rome by the other Christian churches of that time. This is even testified by Gregory the Great himself. Gregory recognized Antioch and Alexandria as Apostolic Sees also exercising "Petrine" authority in the ecclesial *communio* of churches founded by Peter and the other apostles (48, no. 87). Unlike the primacy of jurisdiction, the primacy of honor neither includes an office of universal church leadership nor a ministry of episkopē. The primacy of honor of the Church of Rome, based on the veneration of Peter and Paul as apostles and martyrs and recognized by councils of Constantinople and Chalcedon, is the origin of the papal claim of the primacy of jurisdiction, which was finally dogmatized by Vatican Council I (cf. *Communio Sanctorum: Die Kirche als Gemeinschaft der Heiligen*, issued by the Bilaterale Arbeitsgruppe der Deutschen Bischofskonferenz und der Kirchenleitung der Vereinigten Evangelisch-Lutherischen Kirche Deutschlands [Paderborn: Bonifatius; Frankfurt am Main: Verlag Otto Lembeck, 2000], pp. 81-99, no. 164-200).

argument that the city of Constantinople was younger than the city of Rome. An honorary primacy, even if second-ranking, of the Church of Constantinople was, according to the Council, necessary because the Emperor and Senate were now located there, as had earlier been the case in Rome. In the system of the pentarchy (the major churches of Antioch, Alexandria, Constantinople, Jerusalem, and Rome) the Church of Rome enjoyed an honorary primacy; its bishop was patriarch of the Western church and bore the title *head of the covenant of charity.* The Church of Constantinople and its bishops stood in second place. But it too was endowed with an honorary primacy. In spite of Roman protests,[49] the Bishop of Constantinople bore the title of *Ecumenical Patriarch* (in Latin: *universalis patriarcha*). In sum: in the early church the Church of Rome and its bishops enjoyed an honorary primacy in the period of the imperial church. The unity of the church in its faith was "guaranteed" neither by the Church of Rome nor by that of Constantinople; the common faith was preserved or, in the case of disputes, re-established at ecumenical councils. The individual patriarchates were otherwise independent churches that governed their own affairs independently, but that lived together in communion.

2. Orthodox Churches

184. The Orthodox churches emphasize that the church is at once a local and a universal community. The church preserves its catholicity by forming a real community in each place in the listening to the Word and especially in the celebration of the Eucharist. At the same time it forms a universal people that proclaims the truth of the gospel and overcomes interecclesial disputes. It thus needs conciliar forms that preserve and renew this universal community. Conciliarity is the expression of the communion of the various local churches. Conciliarity finds its expression in councils, representative assemblies that tackle problems and reach solutions that are then binding on the churches, a step found necessary already in the New Testament (the Council of the Apostles in Jerusalem, cf. Acts 15).

185. This conciliar understanding of the one, holy, catholic, and apostolic church is based, according to the Orthodox understanding, on the image and likeness of the triune God, the inner principle of ecclesial communion. Each

---

49. Such as that of Gregory I (595), in *Quellen zur Geschichte des Papsttums und des römischen Katholizismus,* 1st-5th ed., ed. Carl Mirbt, 6th ed., ed. Kurt Aland, vol. 1, *Von den Anfängen bis zum Tridentinum* (Tübingen: J. C. B. Mohr [Paul Siebeck], 1967), pp. 244f., no. 488.

truly Christian local church participates in this communion and is thus part and expression of the mystery of God. It shelters in itself the dynamic of unity that is given by the Holy Spirit.[50] In order to clarify the understanding of the plurality of local churches in the unity of the one church, Orthodoxy puts particular emphasis on the concept of *koinonia,* which conceives of both dimensions of the church not as separate factors, but as two dimensions of a single reality.

186. *Koinonia* describes both God himself and participation in the life of God through Christ in the Holy Spirit. Each member of the church has through baptism a share in this *communio.* Each Eucharist in each local church is the Eucharist of the one church, in which God's *koinonia* is revealed. Starting out from this eucharistic ecclesiological understanding, the question whether the universal church has priority over the local church does not arise. It eliminates a relationship of superior and inferior; theologically, it confirms the simultaneity of local and universal. One must bear this eucharistic underpinning in mind when reflecting on the question of the offices and structures of the Orthodox Church and of the ministry of unity.

187. The ministry of bishop is a significant expression of the simultaneity of local and universal church. The bishop presides over a local church and exercises the ministry of unity in it, a unity that is expressed in the *synaxis* of the Eucharist. The bishop can only exercise his office in the *synaxis* of the local community, and this in turn cannot be a church without the bishop. As the bishop of a local church he is at the same time the bishop of the universal church, as is confirmed by the participation of other bishops in his ordination. The bishop is thus a member of regional and supra-regional synods. Each individual bishop has the right and the duty to take part in them, and is treated as the equal of all the other bishops. The synodal dimension of the episcopal ministry is the expression of the conciliarity of the church. There can be no church without synod or council.

188. The council is first of all the guarantee of the catholicity of the local church. The *koinonia* of the local churches gives its authority to the council or synod. The council cannot interfere in the internal affairs of a local church. The council or synod is therefore not an institution that presides over the local churches, even if each local church must be conscious that its particular decisions are relevant for the universal church. The universal church is the

---

50. Alongside Holy Scripture of the Old and New Testaments, binding on all churches as basis and norm of their faith, in the Orthodox churches the Nicene-Constantinopolitan Creed and the dogmatic pronouncements of the first seven ecumenical councils are binding.

koinonia of the local churches of which no single one alone can be the Catholic Church.

189. A clear understanding of primacy corresponds to this ecclesiology. In theological terms, primacy is always that of the bishop at the level of the local church. As the one who presides over the eucharistic *synaxis* at the local level, his primacy is constitutive for the local church. The *synaxis* of the faithful belongs to this primacy, which in turn is always directed to the *synaxis* of the faithful.

190. What goes for the local church, goes even more so for the regional and universal level. At the regional level, the Metropolitan exercises a primatial ministry in the service of all the local churches. He presides over the synods as *prôtos (primus inter pares)* and is dependent in all his decisions and actions on the assent of all other bishops of the synod. At the level of the patriarchate, too, the patriarch exercises the primatial ministry. The same goes for all patriarchates and autocephalous churches that as part of the universal church subordinate themselves to the conciliar rule of a patriarch as *primus inter pares.*

191. In the first millennium it was unproblematic for the Orthodox patriarchates to recognize the *primus* of the patriarch of Rome. This was underlined anew in a letter of the Patriarch of Constantinople Dimitrios I to Paul VI on December 14, 1975. But for historical and political reasons this function of primacy was transferred to the patriarch of Constantinople following the schism of the eleventh century. The reason for these decisions was the Western claim of a universal primacy of jurisdiction for the Roman patriarchs. According to Orthodox ecclesiology this *primus* of the patriarchs undoubtedly has responsibility for the catholicity of the universal church, but can claim no direct responsibility for the internal affairs of other patriarchates. The Roman claim to primacy of jurisdiction can therefore, from the Orthodox point of view, only be interpreted as placing in question the catholicity and ecclesial integrity of the local churches.

192. That explains why the question of primacy and its exercise represents the decisive obstacle for the unity of the Roman Catholic and Orthodox Church. So far the question has not been tackled in dialogue and only mentioned as "a serious divergence" in the concluding paragraph of the 1988 New Valamo Report of the Joint International Commission for Theological Dialogue between the Roman Catholic Church and the Orthodox Church (GiA II, 679).

3. Anglican Communion

193. A few days after the publication of John Paul II's encyclical *Ut unum sint* the Archbishop of Canterbury, George Carey, Primate of the Anglican Communion, welcomed this document and expressed the basic readiness of his church to examine the ministry of the Bishop of Rome. Two years later the Anglican House of Bishops of England and Wales published a position paper that underlined the agreement that already existed and made recommendations for further dialogue (*May They All Be One*, London 1997). Already the first round of the official international Anglican–Roman Catholic Dialogue (ARCIC I) had led to the first joint Anglican–Roman Catholic statements on the authority in the church and the ministry of the Bishop of Rome. In the first joint statement on *Authority in the Church* (Venice 1976) conciliarity and primacy were underlined as the complementary elements of the *episkopē* and necessary dimensions for the church.

> The bishops are collectively responsible for defending and interpreting the apostolic faith. The primacy accorded to a bishop implies that, after consulting his fellow bishops, he may speak in their name and express their mind. . . . If primacy is to be a genuine expression of *episkopē*, it will foster the *koinonia* by helping the bishops in their task of apostolic leadership both in their local churches and in the Church universal. Primacy fulfils its purpose by helping the churches to listen to one another, to grow in love and unity, and to strive together towards the fullness of Christian life and witness; it respects and promotes Christian freedom and spontaneity; it does not seek uniformity where diversity is legitimate, or centralize administration to the detriment of the local churches. A primate exercises his ministry not in isolation but in collegial association with his brother bishops. (Venice 20 and 21)[51]

194. The second statement on *Authority in the Church* (Windsor 1981) confirmed these basic theological principles. But it also speaks of the continuing divergences between the Roman Catholic and Anglican understanding. These differences especially concern the doctrinal primacy and the jurisdictional primacy, which according to the Catholic understanding are attributable *jure divino* to the Bishop of Rome, a claim that Anglicans cannot share. If these obstacles were to be removed, Anglicans would then see themselves in a posi-

---

51. *GiA* (I), 96.

tion to recognize the particular and historically augmented position of the Bishop of Rome as ministry of unity. This view was confirmed by the whole Anglican Community at the Lambeth Conference in 1988.

195. The outcome of ARCIC II, *The Gift of Authority: Authority in the Church III*, in 1998 further developed these findings and underlined the need for a dialogue on the question of authority in the church. The visible unity of the church depends on consensus in this field. In tackling it, not only an interconfessional problem, but also an important and actual question within the Anglican Communion was addressed. The *Inter-Anglican Theological and Doctrinal Commission* made this clear in the *Virginia Report* presented to the Lambeth Conference in 1998. In this report the question is posed whether the merely consultative (and nonlegislative) character of the worldwide Anglican assemblies would suffice in future for the unity of the church. This question is posed not only in the Anglican Communion, but also in other churches born from the Reformation in the sixteenth century.

196. The ecclesiological foundations of the Anglican Communion largely coincide with the already-outlined Lutheran understanding. The Anglican Communion regards itself as a worldwide communion of churches. The pillars of this communion are consensus in the understanding of the Holy Scriptures of the Old and New Testaments, the importance of the professions of faith in the early church (the Apostles' Creed and the Nicene Creed "as the sufficient statements of the Christian faith"), the recognition of ministries and ordination, in the form of the two sacraments ordained by Christ himself — Baptism and the Lord's Supper — and the historic Episcopate (the so-called Lambeth Quadrilateral). Building on these pillars, the Communion recognizes its duty to seek the visible unity of the church of Jesus Christ.

197. In contrast to the Lutheran position, a special emphasis is laid on the episcopal ministry. The communion of bishops is essential for the unity of the church. The bishops collectively have a personal, collegial, and synodal responsibility for the life, unity, and mission of the church. That a bishop exercises the role of a *primus inter pares* in the college of bishops is not only a historical circumstance, but also a theological need. In this sense it is, in the view of the Anglican Communion, conceivable that the Bishop of Rome could exercise this ministry in a visibly united church. What is at stake in the dialogue with the Roman Catholic Church is not the ministry of the Bishop of Rome, but the present form and exercise of this ministry, especially his claim to primacy in questions of doctrine and jurisdiction, questions that have been touched on in previous ARCIC dialogues, but not yet exhaustively treated.

198. At issue here are not just two particular questions. The understanding

of the ministry of bishop lies behind it. Anglicans and Roman Catholics do not dispute that this ministry is ordained by God and essential for the church, that it has a particular mission for the unity of the local and universal church, and that it is exercised personally, collegially, and synodally. The problem lies in the form of this ministry and in the relation of this particular ministry to the true celebration of Word and Sacrament. Even if Anglicans emphasize the form of the episcopal ministry exercised in their Communion and continually stress in their ecumenical efforts that a commonly exercised episcopal ministry is indispensable for the visible unity of the church, they are also in a position to recognize the true church of Jesus Christ, and the true celebration of word and sacrament, even where this form of episcopal ministry does not exist. The common statements signed by the Anglicans with the Lutheran and Reformed churches of continental Europe (Meissen and Reuilly) confirm that mutual recognition as true church of Jesus Christ does not presuppose the common exercise of the episcopal ministry, but it does imply the duty to strive for this common exercise.

4. Methodist Churches

199. In the Methodist tradition John Wesley, as early as 1744, called annual preaching conferences that had the mission to regulate the doctrine, organization, and practice of the Methodist churches. This rapidly developed into an established *Conference* that comprised roughly a hundred proven Methodist preachers. This office of leadership had the task of recognizing and accompanying the ministry of the preachers. The moderator of the annual *Conference* presided over the celebration for the ordination of new preachers. Due to the rapid expansion of the Methodist churches, geographical districts were established as early as the eighteenth century. These districts were presided over by an elected "chairman," who was a member of the general *Conference* of the Methodist Churches. Since 1878, laypeople were increasingly elected as members of these regional authorities. These various *Conferences* expressed the conciliar character of the Methodist communion and did not have a merely consultative function. Their task was the supervision of the preachers, the formulation and implementation of a synodal discipline, concern for a message true to the Bible, and mission.

200. Even if this form developed at first from an empirical historical situation, it corresponded right from the start to a certain ecclesial understanding that Methodists shared. The church as communion of the faithful requires a

teaching office that is exercised personally, collegially, and synodally. Even if at first Methodists spoke only hesitantly — and in some countries not at all — of an episcopal ministry, they did treat the question of an *episkopē* in theological terms. This ministry was understood as a ministry of unity and sign of the historical continuity of the church. The radical subordination of this *episkopē* to the general authority of Holy Scriptures was always underlined. It was and remains the task of the whole church, to continually examine and formulate anew this ministry on the basis of the teachings of Scripture. The *Ecumenical Methodist Conference,* first convened in 1881, later led to the *World Council of Methodist Churches,* a council that brings together the various national councils. Though it regards itself as the union of communities, it only has an advisory role and has no legislative authority for the churches that are mainly organized at the national level.

201. The questions of church leadership as well as a particular primatial ministry have been discussed in several rounds of dialogue between the World Council of Methodist Churches and the Roman Catholic Church. This took place most clearly in the so-called *Nairobi Report* of 1986 (Towards a Statement on the Church). After initial sections underlining the meaning of the *episkopē* for the church, its doctrine, proclamation, pastoral care, sacraments, and the office of government, this report devoted a chapter to the question of the Petrine ministry. Even if the concept of primacy was at first unfamiliar to them, the Methodists nonetheless acknowledge that "John Wesley exercised a kind of primacy in the origins of the Methodist church. . . . Today's conference continues to embody certain elements of this function" (37). So Methodists are open for a reflection on a universal ministry of unity and on the role that the bishop's see in Rome "might properly exercise in a ministry of universal unity" (40). They see, however, important obstacles in the existing form of the exercise of this ministry in the Roman Catholic Church, especially in the questions of jurisdiction and infallibility (60). With regard to jurisdiction, no orderly and immediate jurisdiction in all dioceses can, in the Methodist understanding, be assigned to the Bishop of Rome (61). Also with regard to the question of infallibility, Methodists have serious reservations — for no man, they believe, can be entitled to determine the truth once and for all. Methodists can always accept "what can clearly be shown to be in agreement with the scriptures" (72). So the question of the form of a universal ministry of unity remains open.[52]

---

52. This was also confirmed in subsequent dialogues: *The Apostolic Tradition,* Singapore 1991 (sections 88-93) and *The Word of Life: A Statement on Revelation and Faith,* Rio de Janeiro 1996 (sections 126-30). See the Nairobi Report in *GiA* II, 583-96.

Chapter IV

Promising Developments and Challenges

202. This chapter, in large measure descriptive, draws attention to important problems dealt with in the broader ecclesiological and ecumenical field, issues highly relevant to the proposals surfaced in the present study on a ministry of unity for the whole church. This survey finds, on the one hand, a number of promising developments (Section A), and on the other, positions that stand in the way of an ecumenical agreement, should they become the dominant perspective for the ecumenical dialogue (Section B). Thus in Section A:

1. the World Conference of Faith and Order of Montreal is recalled, which dealt with a new approach to the understanding of Tradition;
2. the texts of Vatican II's teaching come into focus as to the relationship of Scripture, Tradition, and Magisterium, the latter's ordinary and extraordinary exercise as well as the papacy;
3. the related aspects of the Lutheran/Catholic dialogues since the Malta Report (1972) are summarized, both at the international level (in the Joint Roman Catholic/Evangelical Lutheran Commission, now the Lutheran/Roman Catholic Commission on Unity) and at the national level (in the USA and Germany).

Section B then discusses the viewpoints from Catholic or Lutheran sources that cannot be adopted in common.

A. Promising Developments

1. Montreal 1963: A New Approach to the Concept of Tradition

203. The common recognition of the authority of Holy Scripture as the common foundation of Christian faith is an important feature of the modern ecumenical movement. On the basis of more recent biblical research, theologians came to the insight that Scripture and Tradition cannot be antithetical. This was first expressed clearly at the World Conference of Faith and Order in Montreal in 1963.[1] This conference referred extensively to Catholic theologians like Yves Congar.[2] It explained the Christian Tradition as follows:

> We can say that we exist as Christians by the Tradition of the Gospel (the paradosis of the kerygma) testified in Scripture, transmitted in and by the Church through the power of the Holy Spirit. Tradition taken in this sense is actualised in the preaching of the Word, in the administration of the Sacraments and worship, in Christian teaching and theology, and in mission and witness to Christ by the lives of the members of the Church. What is transmitted in the process of tradition is the Christian faith, not only as a sum of tenets, but as a living reality transmitted through the operation of the Holy Spirit. We can speak of the Christian Tradition (with a capital T), whose content is God's revelation and self-giving in Christ, present in the life of the Church. But this Tradition which is the work of the Holy Spirit is embodied in traditions. . . . The traditions in Christian history are distinct from, and yet connected with, the Tradition. They are the expressions and manifestations in diverse historical forms of the one truth and reality which is Christ. (Montreal 45-47)

204. These diverse historical forms characterize different traditions or confessions, which are influenced and determined by historical, cultural, geographic, and ethnic expressions. Holy Scripture is the written form or witness of the TRADITION, which is interpreted by the Church in ever new situations (Montreal 50). The Conference in Montreal was, however, conscious of a persisting difficulty: namely, what is the criterion that enables us to understand a

---

1. *Documentary History of Faith and Order, 1963-1993,* Faith and Order Paper 159, ed. Günther Gassmann (Geneva: World Council of Churches, 1993), pp. 10-18.

2. See Yves Congar, *La Tradition et les traditions: Essai historique* (Paris: A. Fayard, 1960); Yves Congar, *La Tradition et les traditions: Essai théologique* (Paris: A. Fayard, 1963); Yves Congar, *La Tradition et la vie de l'Église,* 2nd ed. (Paris: Éditions du Cerf, 1984).

tradition as the authentic expression of the TRADITION? "What is 'right interpretation'?" (Montreal 51). This question is answered in different ways by different traditions. At this point the question of the doctrinal ministry is necessarily posed in all Christian traditions. The Conference in Montreal was understandably not in a position to answer this question. The service it did perform, however, was to place in a new light the old question of the relationship between Scripture and Tradition.

2. *The Second Vatican Council:* Dei verbum *and* Lumen gentium

205. The Dogmatic Constitution on Divine Revelation *Dei verbum* is, like that on the church, *Lumen gentium,* the result of various discussions between the "conservative" curial minority party at the Council and the "progressive" majority.[3] In DV Cardinal Ottaviani and Sebastian Tromp wanted Vatican II to endorse the previous prevailing post-tridentine position of the twin sources of divine revelation: Scripture and Tradition. Opposing this position were the conciliar majority under the leadership of Cardinal Bea and Umberto Betti, who wanted to give scope to newer theological insights. The various interpretations show how the final text of the Constitution on Divine Revelation was reached. That such a text came out of the Council at all is thanks to the work of the mixed commission on which both wings of the Council had equal representation. In the face of the opposition between the interpretations represented by both parties, a text was produced that bears the traces of compromise of an unmediated contradictory pluralism;[4] "the final formulations . . . are elastic formulations in all neuralgic points that both sides could inter-

---

3. The discussions themselves need not be described here in detail. This has often been done elsewhere: Joseph Ratzinger, "Einleitung zu 'Dei verbum' und Kommentar zu DV Ch. I, II and VI," in *LThK,* Erg.-Bd. II (Freiburg, Basel, Vienna: Herder, 1967), pp. 498-528 and 571-81; Alois Grillmeier, "Einleitung und Kommentar zu DV, Ch. III," in *LThK,* Erg.-Bd. II, pp. 528-58; Béda Rigaux, "Einleitung und Kommentar zu DV, Ch. IV and V," in *LThK,* Erg.-Bd. II, pp. 558-70; Otto Hermann Pesch, *Das Zweite Vatikanische Konzil: Vorgeschichte — Verlauf — Ergebnisse — Nachgeschichte,* 2nd ed. (Würzburg: Echter Verlag, 1994), pp. 271-90; Helmut Hoping, "Theologischer Kommentar zur Dogmatischen Konstitution 'Dei Verbum,'" in *Herders Theologischer Kommentar zum Zweiten Vatikanischen Konzil,* vol. 3, ed. Peter Hünermann and Bernd Jochen Hilberath (Freiburg, Basel, Vienna: Herder, 2005), pp. 695-831.

4. M. Seckler, "Über den Kompromiss in Sachen der Lehre," in *Begegnung: Beiträge zu einer Hermeneutik des theologischen Gesprächs,* FS Heinrich Fries, ed. Max Seckler, Otto Hermann Pesch, Johannes Brosseder, and Wolfhart Pannenberg (Graz, Vienna, Cologne: Styria, 1972), pp. 45-57, here 57.

pret each according to its tastes — and indeed did so in the following period."[5]

206. One of the goals of Vatican II, it should be recalled, was "to encourage whatever can contribute to the union of all who believe in Christ" (SC 1). In this sense the Council was also called to clarify the relation between Scripture, Tradition, Church, and teaching office. Important statements of DV were not, and are not, bones of contention between the churches: before it was consigned to Scripture, Divine Revelation was transmitted by the preaching of Jesus himself and the oral preaching of the apostles and disciples after the crucifixion and resurrection. This apostolic tradition had its fallout in the plurality of their witnesses in Scripture. That the canon of Scripture arose in the church is uncontested. That Scripture was and is read and understood in the church is equally uncontested.

207. DV 9 establishes that "sacred tradition and sacred scripture are bound closely together and communicate one with the other. They both flow from the same divine wellspring." "Tradition and scripture make up a single sacred deposit of the word of God" (DV 10); "Thus it is that the church does not draw its certainty about all revealed truths from the holy scriptures alone. Hence, both scripture and tradition must be accepted and honored with equal devotion and reverence" (DV 9). In DV 10 the Council says that "the task of giving an authentic interpretation of the word of God, whether in its written form or in the form of tradition, has been entrusted to the living teaching office of the church alone." Admittedly, in this same paragraph (DV 10) it is said that "[t]his magisterium is not superior to the word of God, but is rather its servant. It teaches only what has been handed on to it. At the divine command and with the help of the Holy Spirit, it listens to this devoutly, guards it reverently and expounds it faithfully." Yet in the same section of the Constitution (DV 10) it is affirmed that "tradition, scripture and the magisterium of the church are so connected and associated that one of them cannot stand without the others. Working together, each in its own way the action of the one holy Spirit, they all contribute effectively to the salvation of souls."

208. According to DV 8,

This tradition that comes from the apostles makes progress in the church with the help of the holy Spirit. There is a growth in insight into the realities and words that are being passed on. This comes about through con-

5. Pesch, *Das Zweite Vatikanische Konzil*, p. 283.

templation and study by believers who "ponder these things in their hearts" (see Luke, 2:19 and 51). It comes from the intimate sense of spiritual realities which they experience. And it comes from the preaching of those who, on succeeding to the office of bishop, have received the sure charism of truth.

209. In determining the intention of the sacred writers, exegetes must make use of the methods of critical historical interpretation and the analysis of literary forms of expression "in order that their research may help the church's judgment to mature" (DV 12). In this research, attention must be paid to the content and unity of the whole of Scripture, taking into account the living tradition of the entire church and the analogy of faith.

210. In chapter VI of DV it is affirmed:

The church has always venerated the divine scriptures as it has venerated the Body of the Lord. . . . The church has always regarded and continues to regard the scriptures, taken together with sacred tradition, as the supreme rule of its faith. For since they are inspired by God and committed to writing once and for all time, they present God's own word in an unalterable form, and they make the voice of the holy Spirit sound again and again in the words of the prophets and the apostles. It follows that all the preaching of the church, as indeed the entire christian religion, should be nourished and ruled by sacred scripture. (DV 21)

211. And a little further on we read:

Sacred theology relies on the written word of God, taken together with sacred tradition, as its permanent foundation. By this word it is powerfully strengthened and constantly rejuvenated. . . . The sacred scriptures contain the word of God, and, because they are inspired, they truly are the word of God; therefore the study of the sacred page should be the very soul of theology. (DV 24)

212. The texts cited both underline Scripture, the written Word of God, as the highest standard of faith, as the lodestar of the church and its preaching, and also as the foundation and soul of theology.

213. Despite significant advances in several statements of DV that clearly testify to the normativity of Holy Scripture in relation to the doctrinal tradition of the church, one finds other passages where this clarity is missing. Such passages so yoke Scripture, Tradition, and Magisterium together that an ob-

jection appealing to Scripture over against tradition and the teaching office is not possible. When one takes the text of DV as a whole, open questions remain in regard to the relationship between the apostolic tradition as found deposited in Scripture, and the post-apostolic teaching tradition of the church. (Trent treated the latter as oral apostolic tradition that comes down to us by way of bishops' sees and the teaching office.)

214. Otto Hermann Pesch, in his examination of DV, drew the following conclusions:

> The greatest service of the Constitution on Divine Revelation is to have left open, i.e. made no decision about, the question about Scripture and Tradition and their relation to the teaching office in all decisive questions — exactly as at the Council of Trent. In the face of the idea of a "pre-established harmony" between Scripture, Tradition and teaching office, represented [at Vatican II] — in contrast to Trent — only by a minority, but supported by official church theory and practice, this was the most that was achievable: to have texts which could be appealed to if someone were of another opinion than "Rome" or "other teaching offices."[6]

215. In LG the doctrine of the church's teaching office is embedded in that of the church and its constitution.[7] The teaching office is in the hands of the bishops as the teachers and pastors of their local churches (though individually they do not have infallibility), and of the whole body of bishops along with the papacy and the pope. A distinction is drawn between the *ordinary magisterium,* expressed in encyclicals, decrees, statements, admonitions, addresses, pastoral letters, catechisms, and so forth, and the *extraordinary magisterium,* bindingly expressed in solemn *ex cathedra* pronouncements by the pope, in solemn conciliar decrees (councils), and in doctrine agreed upon by all the bishops and the pope.

216. In LG the doctrine of the church's teaching office can be found in the part dealing with the church's hierarchical structure (chapter III), which in the main follows the traditional line. As successors of the apostles, *bishops* have the Lord's commission to teach all nations and to proclaim the gospel to every creature (LG 24). In this respect the body of bishops, the college of bishops, only has authority *in conjunction, and only if united with the Bishop of Rome* as Peter's successor and head of the college.

---

6. Pesch, *Das Zweite Vatikanische Konzil,* p. 289.

7. On the relation of Vatican II to Vatican I, see above, Chapters II and III.B.

[T]he Roman Pontiff has . . . full, supreme and universal power over the whole church, a power which he can always exercise freely. The order of bishops is successor to the college of the apostles . . . and in it the apostolic college is perpetuated. Together with its head, the Supreme Pontiff, and never apart from him, it is the subject of supreme and full power over the universal church; but this power cannot be exercised without the consent of the Roman pontiff. (LG 22)

217. The bishops are "authentic teachers, that is, teachers endowed with the authority of Christ" (LG 25), and they are to be honored as witnesses to divine and catholic truth. Believers must consent to a statement of their bishop on doctrinal and moral matters that is uttered in Christ's name and show it a religiously based obedience (LG 25). Furthermore,

(t)his religious docility of will and intellect must be extended in a special way to the authentic teaching authority of the Roman Pontiff, even when he does not speak *ex cathedra*; in such wise, indeed, that his supreme teaching authority be acknowledged with respect, and that one sincerely adhere to decisions made by him conformably with his manifest mind and intention. . . . (LG 25)

218. The pope enjoys *infallibility* when, "as supreme pastor and teacher of all the faithful, . . . he proclaims in a definitive act a doctrine pertaining to faith or morals. For that reason, his definitions are rightly said to be irreformable by their very nature, and not by reason of the consent of the church . . ." (LG 25).

219. The bishops also enjoy such *infallibility* when as a college, and in agreement with the pope, they unanimously and definitively issue a specific judgment on a matter of faith and morals. This is especially the case when they do so in an *ecumenical* council. The doctrine to be defined is set forth in accordance with revelation itself.

This revelation is transmitted in its entirety either in written form or in oral tradition through the legitimate succession of bishops and above all through the care of the Roman Pontiff himself; and through the light of the Spirit of truth it is scrupulously preserved in the church and unerringly explained. . . . However, they do not admit any new public revelation as pertaining to the divine deposit of faith. (LG 25)

3. Lutheran-Catholic Theological Dialogue

220. The Lutheran tradition does not recognize the exercise of the teaching office centered on one person. The Lutheran Confessions issued in the sixteenth century have value as *norma normata,* as binding interpretation of the *norma normans* of holy Scripture. Pastors, both men and women, are pledged by their ordination to abide by holy Scripture and the Confessions of the church. New teaching developments are possible and lie in the hand of synods. In this regard it should be underlined that the teaching authority in the individual churches has taken on different form in the individual churches (episcopal-synodal structures; presbyteral-synodal structures).

3.1. The First International Lutheran-Catholic Dialogue

221. The first official international Lutheran-Catholic dialogue led to the so-called *Malta Report* in 1972.[8] Its first chapter is devoted to the question about the gospel and its transmission. It is established at the outset that the relationship between Scripture and Tradition "poses the old controversial question . . . in a new way" (Malta, no. 17). As in the above-mentioned World Conference of *Faith and Order* in Montreal (1963) it is added that the decisive "question of the criteria by means of which one may distinguish between legitimate and illegitimate later developments . . . cannot be answered in a purely theoretical manner" (no. 18). In order to make progress here, a distinction is drawn between "primary" and "secondary" criteria:

> Neither the *sola scriptura* [principle] nor formal references to the authoritativeness of the magisterial office are sufficient. The primary criterion is the Holy Spirit making the Christ event into a saving action. To be sure, this raises the question of how the power of the Holy Spirit can be concretely identified as criterion. If the continuity of tradition with its original source is to be concretely manifest, then obviously secondary criteria are necessary. (no. 18)

222. The primary criterion is the absolute authority of the gospel "as proclamation of God's saving action . . . (and) therefore itself a salvation event" (no. 16) and its priority over Scripture, church, dogma, and teaching office, whereby Scripture "as the witness to the fundamental tradition . . . has a normative role

8. *GiA* (I), 168-89.

for the entire later tradition of the church" (no. 17). "The authority of the church can only be service of the word and . . . is not master of the word of the Lord" (no. 21).

223. The differentiation between primary and secondary criteria leads to a critical question posed to both parties. Lutherans are asked what in their tradition is the true authority of the secondary criteria, to which they answer by reference to the meaning of the confessions of the church: "The Confessions of the Church possess authority as a correct interpretation of Scripture" (no. 19). Catholics are asked to explain how in their tradition the final authority of the gospel is made clear in relation to church and teaching office. In their answer they point to "the reciprocal interaction of official and unofficial charisma, both of which remain under Scripture" (no. 20).

224. This first report of the international Lutheran-Catholic dialogue is characterized by the attempt to relativize the "secondary criteria." These criteria "must remain open to the word [of God] and must transmit it in such a way that the word constantly bestows the understanding which comes from faith and freedom of Christian action" (no. 21). Both partners "are convinced that the Holy Spirit unceasingly leads and keeps the church in the truth. It is in this context that one must understand the concepts of indefectibility and infallibility which are current in the Catholic tradition" (no. 22).

225. In spite of clear signs of rapprochement, however, the questions posed in Montreal about the criteria that permit us to understand a tradition as an authentic expression of the TRADITION could not yet be answered in this first phase of the international dialogue.

3.2. The Lutheran-Catholic Dialogue in the USA

226. Already prior to the conclusion of the Second Vatican Council, Lutheran churches in the USA had got into contact with the Catholic Church, and after introductory dialogues on the Nicene Creed as dogma of the Church (1965) and on baptism (1966) Catholics and Lutherans noted a remarkable and growing agreement regarding the sacrificial character of the Eucharist as well as a unanimity in the understanding of the real presence, although this was expressed in different terms. In addition, Catholic participants in the dialogue on *Eucharist and Ministry* (1970) recommended — although not without subsequent criticism from their own ranks — recognizing the validity of the ordained Lutheran ministry and by implication also the presence of the body and blood of Jesus Christ in the Lord's Supper of the Lutheran churches.

227. The considerations of the American dialogue group on the papal primacy and the universal church[9] (published 1974) concentrated on the Petrine function as *"a particular form of Ministry exercised by a person, officeholder, or local church with reference to the church as a whole"* with the assignment "to promote or preserve the oneness of the church by symbolizing unity, and by facilitating communication, mutual assistance or correction, and collaboration in the church's mission."[10] Although such a ministry in principle can be exercised by various instances and throughout history has in fact been held by different officeholders (bishops, patriarchs, church presidents), the fact remains that "the single most notable representative of this Ministry toward the church universal, both in duration and geographical scope, has been the bishop of Rome," and it is added that "(t)he Reformers did not totally reject all aspects of the papal expression of the Petrine function, but only what they regarded as its abuses."[11]

228. As a consequence, the Lutheran participants were confronted with the challenge, whether a more pastorally than juridically orientated papacy, renewed in the light of the gospel and committed to Christian freedom and open to other confessional traditions, would be legitimate not only in the Roman Catholic Church, but could also be possible and desirable within a greater community, *in casu* even embracing Lutheranism. On the other side, the Catholic participants understood the dialogue result as a convergence, which made a reconciliation with Lutheranism possible and paved the road to a new understanding of the Lutheran churches as "sister-churches which are already entitled to some measure of ecclesiastical communion" — for whom an official fellowship with the Church of Rome may even call for "a distinct canonical status."[12]

229. To begin with, the dialogue on primacy had left out the connected issue of papal infallibility as an area with its own concepts and recent historical development. The group logically turned to infallibility, then, after having completed the reflections on primacy, thus continuing the U.S. dialogue with the report on *Teaching Authority & Infallibility in the Church*.[13] More than three

---

9. Paul C. Empie and Thomas Austin Murphy, eds., *Papal Primacy and the Universal Church*, Lutherans and Catholics in Dialogue V (Minneapolis: Augsburg, 1974).

10. *Papal Primacy and the Universal Church*, Common Statement, par. 4, pp. 11-12.

11. *Papal Primacy and the Universal Church*, Common Statement, par. 5, p. 12.

12. *Papal Primacy and the Universal Church*, Common Statement, par. 33, p. 23; cf. no. 38.

13. Paul C. Empie, Thomas Austin Murphy, and Joseph A. Burgess, eds., *Teaching Authority & Infallibility in the Church*, Lutherans and Catholics in Dialogue VI (Minneapolis: Augsburg, 1978).

decades ago the American theologians also here achieved remarkable rapprochements and, even in the perspective of a later generation, highly surprising convergences.

230. The Catholic participants understand the result of the dialogue on infallibility as a contribution toward a critical reassessment of the traditional theological interpretation of the dogma of 1870. This could make it possible for the Lutheran partners not to exclude primacy and doctrinal authority of the pope under all circumstances, but to comprehend it as an expression of the indefectibility of the church.[14] The ministry of the Bishop of Rome has to be seen as a service to the word of God and under its authority, and the doctrine on infallibility is "an expression of confidence that the Spirit of God abides in his church and guides it in the truth."[15] The dialogue group is convinced that such a renewed understanding of a formerly most controversial doctrine could build up a *magisterial mutuality,* which — while acknowledging the presence of the Spirit of Christ in the Catholic as well as in the Lutheran Church — would make possible common teaching, would promote the development of a common public witness, and would recognize priests as well as pastors as partners in the proclamation of the gospel.

3.3. *The Dialogue in Germany between the DBK and the VELKD*

231. A more precise elucidation of this problem was later produced in the bilateral working group of the German Catholic Bishops' Conference (DBK) and the Council of the VELKD (United Evangelical Lutheran Church of Germany), which published its findings in 2000 under the title *Communio Sanctorum: Die Kirche als Gemeinschaft der Heiligen* [the Church as Communion of Saints].[16]

---

14. "The context within which the Catholic doctrine of papal infallibility is understood has changed. Lutherans and Catholics now speak in increasingly similar ways about the gospel and its communication, about the authority of Christian truth, and about how to settle disputes concerning the understanding of the Christian message. One can truly speak of a convergence between our two traditions." *Teaching Authority & Infallibility in the Church,* Common Statement, par. 41, p. 30.

15. *Teaching Authority & Infallibility in the Church,* Common Statement, par. 53, p. 36. "This understanding should allay Lutheran fears that papal infallibility is a usurpation of the sovereign authority of Christ, and make clear that this dogma is not the central doctrine of the Catholic Church and that it does not displace Christ from his redemptive and mediatorial role."

16. Bilaterale Arbeitsgruppe der Deutschen Bischofskonferenz und der Kirchenleitung der Vereinigten Evangelisch-Lutherischen Kirche Deutschlands, *Communio Sanctorum: Die Kirche als Gemeinschaft der Heiligen* (Paderborn: Bonifatius; Frankfurt am Main: Verlag Otto Lembeck, 2000).

232. The starting point is the revelation as self-communication of God, which has its culmination and fulfillment in Jesus Christ. This revelation founds the Christian faith, which recognizes the Word of God through the Holy Spirit. The biblical Scriptures testify to God's voice and action in the history of his people Israel and in the history of Jesus of Nazareth. In the words of the Scriptures the living voice of God can be heard ever anew and continues in perpetuity to have its effect. The "witness of the first witnesses" happened within the community of the church.

> The Church lives from the Word of God and is at the same time placed in its service. . . . She fulfils (her service) by referring to the truth of Christ, to Christ as Truth itself. The Church has the promise of the Holy Spirit that guides her in the truth. . . . It is not granted to the Church to do what she wants with the truth. Insofar as the Church is taken into this service as the witness of truth, she speaks . . . with full authority. She is consequently the addressee of the Revelation and at the same time the bearer of its universal transmission. As mediator the Church also faces each individual believer. But she derives her full authority not from herself, but from the Word of God which she proclaims.[17]

233. In this fundamental consensus the various authorities of witness *(Bezeugungsinstanzen)* are therefore bound together in dialogue, for agreement on the authority of Holy Scripture demands an agreement on their cooperation. These various authorities of witness are listed: the Holy Scripture as original witness of the truth of the living God, the transmission of the faith *(Tradition)*, the witness of the whole people of God *(the believers' instinct of faith, Glaubenssinn)*, the teaching office of the church, and theology. A particular role is ascribed to Holy Scripture, since it attests to the Word of God, which alone is binding (no. 46-50). The Tradition brings no addition in terms of content to Holy Scripture, but Scripture is necessarily dependent on this process of Tradition.[18]

17. Die Kirche lebt aus dem Wort Gottes und ist zugleich in dessen Dienst gestellt . . . , indem sie auf die Wahrheit Christi verweist, auf Christus als die Wahrheit selbst. Die Kirche hat die Verheissung des Heiligen Geistes, der sie in der Wahrheit leitet. . . . Der Kirche ist es nicht gegeben, über die Wahrheit zu verfügen. . . . Insofern die Kirche in diesen Dienst der Bezeugung der Wahrheit genommen ist, spricht sie . . . in Vollmacht. Sie ist folglich Adressat der Offenbarung und gleichzeitig Trägerin ihrer universalen Vermittlung. Als Vermittlerin steht die Kirche den einzelnen Glaubenden auch gegenüber. Sie hat ihre Vollmacht aber nicht von sich selbst, sondern vom Wort Gottes, das sie verkündigt" (no. 43-44).

18. The "transmission of the witness of revelation . . . connects . . . the experiences, findings

234. After a precise description of the authorities of witness, in which many "fundamental agreements" exist, the dialogue proceeds to "the still unresolved controversy with regard to the bearers of the teaching office."[19] Here the problem revolves not around the question of infallibility as such, but around the determination of the relation between the various authorities of witness.[20]

235. Under the heading *Petrine ministry, Communio Sanctorum* deals extensively with the issue of papal primacy (no. 153-200) that has so far been treated as separate subject only in the American Lutheran-Catholic Dialogue 1974, to which the German text explicitly refers.[21] The report treats issues concerning the role of Peter in the New Testament and the early church (no. 158-63) that implied functions of a universal teaching and pastoral ministry, serving to further the unity of all the communities (no. 163); then it provides a description of the historical development of the primacy up to Vatican II (no. 164-75). This leads up to an account of the critical attitude of the reformers over against papacy (no. 176-80) as well as of the current Protestant questions and reflections on the issue (no. 181-91). Conclusions for Catholics as well as for Lutherans are drawn toward the end of the document (no. 192-94). The result of the deliberations is summarized as follows:

---

and discoveries that the church in her history has made in relation to the Word of God both in thought and life" (no. 55). "The Tradition . . . constantly needs critical interpretation, however much it is itself a critical authority for the church" (no. 56). With regard to the teaching office the document stresses "that there is a compulsory nature of Christian doctrine that is binding on the church and that in both Churches a responsibility for doctrine is incumbent on the ordained ministry both at the community and at the supra-community level; . . . responsibility for teaching (is) an integral part of the witness of faith of the whole Church, and . . . binding doctrine is subject to the norm of the Gospel" (no. 61).

19. This controversy concerns the question whether this is expressed by the church as a whole in an infallible way, or whether it is mediated through particular structures (college of bishops, council, pope), which have been established in the church through Christ and therefore under certain conditions can make infallible decisions (no. 63).

20. "The interaction of the 'authorities of witness' as described above can only succeed through the work of the Holy Spirit and cannot be understood without its intervention." In spite of this declaration, the document comes to the conclusion that "the respective interaction of the individual authorities of witness even within the churches (remains) not without tensions and conflicts and therefore stands in need of a system of rules" (no. 73). This is all the more the case in interconfessional relations; neither was this German dialogue really able to resolve the open questions as stated in the Malta Report.

21. In other international Lutheran-Catholic dialogues the issue of primacy is only dealt with within the framework of other subjects: "Ways to Community" (1980), *GiA* (I), 215ff.; "The Ministry in the Church" (1981), *GiA* (I), 248ff.; "Facing Unity" (1984), *GiA* II, 443ff.; "Church and Justification" (1995), *GiA* II, 485ff., here no. 106.

In common with one another, Catholics and Lutherans can state (no. 195): A universal church ministry for the unity and the truth of the church corresponds to the essence and mission of the church, which constitutes itself at the local, regional, and universal levels. Such a ministry has to be seen therefore in principle as objectively appropriate. It represents the entirety of Christianity and has a pastoral task toward all particular churches (no. 196). This ministry is obligated to remain true to the biblical Word and to the binding Tradition of the church. It is necessarily tied into the structures that give form to *communio,* imprinted as they are by conciliarity, collegiality, and subsidiarity (no. 197). Shared insights of this kind leave considerable room for various models in regard to particular questions of a theological, historical, and canonical nature. This applies e.g. to the question whether the historical Jesus founded a Petrine ministry, when and how such a ministry took shape, and how the functions of this office accrued to the Bishop of Rome. Other questions can also remain open in the realm of the political, canonical, and historically conditioned development and solidification of the Petrine ministry (no. 198). Problems weighing against agreement arise from the determinations of the First Vatican Council as to the primacy of jurisdiction and the infallibility of the pope. The principle of the juridical primacy is not acceptable for Lutheran thought, unless it is firmly and legally imbedded in the *communio* structure of the church. Similarly the principle of infallibility is not acceptable for a Lutheran understanding, unless even *ex cathedra* judgments of the pope are subject to an ultimate proviso by reason of the revelation given in Holy Scripture.[22]

---

22. "Gemeinsam können Katholiken und Lutheraner sagen: (no. 195) Ein universalkirchlicher Dienst an der Einheit und der Wahrheit der Kirche entspricht dem Wesen und Auftrag der Kirche, die sich auf lokaler, regionaler und universaler Ebene verwirklicht. Er ist daher grundsätzlich als sachentsprechend anzusehen. Dieser Dienst repräsentiert die gesamte Christenheit und hat eine pastorale Aufgabe an allen Teilkirchen. (no. 196) Dieser Dienst ist der Treue zum biblischen Wort sowie der verbindlichen Tradition der Kirche verpflichtet. Er ist notwendigerweise eingebunden in Strukturen, in denen die *communio* Gestalt findet. Diese werden geprägt durch Konziliarität, Kollegialität und Subsidiarität. (no. 197) Solche gemeinsamen Einsichten lassen Raum für unterschiedliche Auffassungen hinsichtlich theologischer, historischer und kirchenrechtlicher Einzelfragen. Das betrifft z.B. die Frage, ob der historische Jesus ein Petrusamt gestiftet hat, wann und wie ein solches ausgebildet worden ist oder wie die Funktionen dieses Amtes dem Bischof von Rom zugekommen sind. Offen bleiben können auch die Fragen nach der politischen, kirchenrechtlichen und historisch bedingten Ausgestaltung und Konkretisierung des Petrusdienstes. (no. 198) Probleme der Verständigung ergeben sich angesichts der Festlegungen des Ersten Vatikanischen Konzils über den *Jurisdiktionsprimat* und die *Unfehlbarkeit* des Papstes: Das Prinzip des *Jurisdiktionsprimates* ist für lutherisches

236. The Catholic participants consider these hesitations to be legitimate and argue that the primacy of jurisdiction also according to Catholic doctrine must be understood within the *communio* structure of the church (cf. LG 13). Furthermore, they are convinced that papal infallibility can only be exercised in absolute fidelity to apostolic faith and Holy Scripture (cf. LG 25) in such a way that a pope who would not observe this fidelity would *eo ipso* lose his office.

237. Both dialogue partners would welcome it, if such an interpretation could become the official stance of the church (no. 198). A reconciliation concerning the Petrine ministry can only be understood as conversion *(Umkehr und Bekehrung)* and a new beginning of universal communion on the basis of traditions that are at home in all churches. All churches share this task. A universal unity including participation of all Christians would imply the mutual recognition of the participating churches, a common understanding of the apostolic faith, a communion of sacraments, and a mutual recognition of those ministries entrusted with Word and sacraments. This context gives rise to the question, if and to what extent the papacy in its actual historical shape has kept the true and indispensable core of the Petrine ministry (no. 200). In addition, the Roman Catholic Church is confronted with the problem, if and to what extent it would be basically possible to create between non-Catholic churches and the Holy See a form of communion, in which the very being of the Petrine care for unity is preserved, though this would be exercised according to canonical rules and standards other than those that have been valid since the Middle Ages and especially in the modern period. The following considerations may serve as incentives to continue the dialogue on this issue:

- the possibility of using as an orientation the way in which primacy was exercised in the first Christian millennium, as standard, irrespective of later developments;
- the differentiation of ministries accumulated in the person of the pope: Bishop of Rome, Pastor of the Universal Church, Head of the College of Bishops, Primate of Italy, Archbishop and Metropolitan of the Church Province of Rome, Sovereign of the *Città del Vaticano;*

Verständnis nicht akzeptabel, wenn nicht seine Ausgestaltung die Einbindung in die *Communio*-Struktur der Kirche rechtlich verpflichtend vorschreibt. Das Prinzip der *Unfehlbarkeit* ist ebenfalls für lutherisches Verständnis nicht akzeptabel, wenn nicht auch "*Excathedra*"-Entscheidungen des Papstes einem letzten Vorbehalt durch die in der Heiligen Schrift gegebene Offenbarung unterliegen."

- the shaping of the church as a *communio* of sister churches;
- the development of the relationship between the Church of Rome and the Eastern Catholic churches;
- the legitimate diversity in liturgy, theology, spirituality, leadership, and practice.

3.4. The International Lutheran-Catholic Dialogue on Apostolicity

238. The study document of the Lutheran/Roman Catholic Commission on Unity, *The Apostolicity of the Church*,[23] delves in its fourth part ("Church doctrine that remains in the truth") into the question of Scripture and Tradition. Here it is jointly declared that for Catholics and Lutherans Scripture is "the source, rule, guideline, and criterion of correctness and purity of the church's proclamation, of its elaboration of doctrine, and of its sacramental and pastoral practice" (no. 434). The fundamental reason for this is that the New Testament writings arose in the first communities through the proclamation of the apostles under the inspiration of the Holy Spirit. They should — together with the sacred books of Israel in the Old Testament — "make present for all ages the truth of God's word, so as to form faith and guide believers in a life worthy of the gospel of Christ" (no. 434). It therefore can and must be jointly confessed: "By the biblical canon, the church does not constitute, but instead recognizes, the inherent authority of the prophetic and apostolic Scriptures" (no. 434).

> When Catholics affirm that tradition is indispensable in the interpretation of the word of God . . . , they are connecting the gospel and Scripture with the Christian faith lived and transmitted in history [of the church], where transmission has given rise to valid expressions of that faith. (no. 443)

239. Here what Catholics have in mind are the rules of faith, the confessions of faith, above all that of Nicea-Constantinople, and the conciliar formulations of the articles of faith. These claim to be "concentrated summaries and clarifications of what is announced in the apostolic gospel and documented in the books of Scripture," and should therefore "as fundamental expressions of faith and life . . . orient church teaching and biblical interpretation" (no. 443).

---

23. *The Apostolicity of the Church: Study Document of the Lutheran–Roman Catholic Commission on Unity,* ed. The Lutheran World Federation and Pontifical Council for Promoting Christian Unity (Minneapolis: Lutheran University Press, 2006). — German edition: *Die Apostolizität der Kirche: Studiendokument der Lutherisch/Römisch-katholischen Kommission für die Einheit* (Paderborn: Bonifatius; Frankfurt am Main: Verlag Otto Lembeck, 2009).

Understood in this way, *Tradition* comes close to the role played by the confessions of the early church and the Confessions of the Reformation in the Lutheran churches. The reformers regarded these Confessions as founded in Holy Scripture and as summations that would guide the further interpretation of Scripture and protect it from false teaching (cf. no. 446).

240. The Catholic side for its part makes the distinction:

> The many "traditions" are the forms of life and practice which apply God's word and are observed out of fidelity to the community of faith. Scripture *is* the inspired word of God, while tradition is the living process which "*transmits* in its entirety the Word of God entrusted to the apostles by Christ and the Holy Spirit" (DV 9). This transmission is not the source of new truths by which the content of inspired Scripture would be supplemented, but it does give rise to the elementary expressions . . . , which are not simply "human traditions," for they express and render certain the biblical content of faith. (no. 444)

241. Even if Lutherans acknowledge the belonging together of Scripture and Tradition (Confession), they equally stress that "Scripture should not be absorbed into the tradition-process, but should remain permanently superior as a critical norm" (no. 447). The Commission sees in the field of Scripture and Tradition "such an extensive agreement that their different emphases do not of themselves require maintaining the present division of the churches. In this area, there is unity in reconciled diversity" (no. 448).

242. In the present doctrine of the churches, Scripture and Tradition are subject to the shifting challenges of the present and therefore must always be brought anew into the right relation to each other. As far as the teaching office is concerned, a clear asymmetry exists between the Roman Catholic Church and the Lutheran churches, which the document distinguishes in linguistic terms by speaking of *service of teaching* in the Lutheran churches and *teaching office* in the Roman Catholic Church.

> In Catholic ecclesiology "magisterium" designates the mission of teaching that is proper to the episcopal college, to the Pope as its head, and to individual bishops linked in hierarchical communion with the successor of Peter. (no. 452)

243. In the Lutheran churches, by contrast, the service of teaching is exercised both at the local level in sermons and in the teaching of pastors as also

at the supra-regional level by superintendents or bishops and synods, to which the nonordained also belong. This service

> must not focus exclusively on office-holders and institutions, but also take account of the processes of interactions between office-holders, of interventions by Christians practicing the common priesthood of the baptized, and of theologians who contribute the results of their scholarly study and conclusions on doctrinal questions. Lutheran churches earnestly hope that through these processes the Holy Spirit is maintaining them in the truth of the gospel. . . . (no. 451)

244. Lutherans and Catholics say that without a teaching office the church would suffer from a lack in the transmission of the gospel. Each office is exercised in a "network of several instances of witness" (no. 457) that is understood in theologically different ways in the churches and also institutionally ordered in different ways. On the journey of the church through time the teaching ministry has the task "to give public voice in an ongoing manner to the definitive coming of God" (no. 460).

245. On the supposition that the promising beginnings, evident in the separate documents examined here in Section A, get developed further, then an ecumenical agreement in these important issues could result. Some might prune back what is exaggerated, or in Eberhard Jüngel's expression, dismantle the "menacing 'too much,' "[24] while others might rediscover what has been overlooked or underestimated until now.

B. Problematic Developments

1. The Controversy over the Ecclesiological Status of Lutheran Churches

246. Four documents of the *Congregation for the Doctrine of the Faith* are incompatible with the concept of the unity of the church as a communion of churches. These documents stand in need of a completely new ecclesiological orientation; their fundamental perspective has to be transformed into an ec-

---

24. "Das bedrohliche Zuviel" in Eberhard Jüngel, "Kirche im eigentlichen Sinn: Wie soll der Protestantismus auf die Anmaßung aus Rom reagieren?" (2007), *Neue Zürcher Zeitung* (www.nzz.ch/nachrichten/kultur//aktuell/kirche_im_eigentlichen_sinn_1.527265.html; *NZZ online,* October 12, 2009). See also the following section B.1.

clesiology of a real *communio ecclesiarum*. The *communio* ecclesiology of the Second Vatican Council should be the starting point of its development. This development has not yet taken place. These four documents are:[25]

- Letter to the bishops of the Catholic Church on some aspects of the church understood as communion — *Communionis notio* (28 May 1992);[26]
- *Note on the expression "Sister churches"*: A letter to the presidents of the conferences of bishops (30 June 2000);[27]
- *Declaration "Dominus Iesus" on the unicity and salvific universality of Jesus Christ and the church* (6 August 2000; published 5 September 2000);[28]
- *Responses to some questions regarding certain aspects of the doctrine on the church* (29 June 2007).[29]

247. What would substantially stand in the way of any ecumenical convergence, should they in fact determine future Roman Catholic ecumenical endeavors, are the following positions:

a) The Roman Catholic Church is the Mother Church and cannot have any sisters on this level of her maternity. The Orthodox Patriarchates could be sister churches only on the level of Roman Catholic particular or else local churches (dioceses). That means: The Ecumenical Patriarchate of Constantinople could only be a sister of, e.g., the metropolitan archdiocese of Rome or Milan, but not a sister of the Roman Catholic Church. The Protestant churches can in no way be called sister churches, because they are not churches in the proper sense of the term "church."

b) The unity of the church of Jesus Christ is given from its first beginnings within the Roman Catholic Church. The lack of the unity among Christians, to be sure, is a deep wound for the Roman Catholic Church, which hinders the full realization of the universality of the Roman Catholic Church in history (cf. *Dominus Iesus*, no. 17).

25. On the authority of Roman Catholic documents, see above, Chapter III.B.2 Appendix.

26. *AAS* 85 (1993): 838-50.

27. www.vatican.va/roman_curia/congregations/cfaith/documents/rc_con_cfaith_doc _20000630_chiese-sorelle_en.html; see also "Nota sull'espressione 'Chiese sorelle,'" *L'Osservatore Romano*, October 28, 2000, p. 6.

28. *AAS* 92 (2000), 742-65.

29. www.vatican.va/roman_curia/congregations/cfaith/documents/rc_con_cfaith_doc _20070629_responsa-quaestiones_en.html

c) The fullness of the church of Jesus Christ is only realized in the Roman Catholic Church. All the other Christian churches and ecclesial communities are suffering from ecclesiological *defectus:* the Orthodox churches are not living in communion with Rome, and within the ecclesial communities of the Reformation one can only see elements of sanctification and of truth, which as proper gifts of the church of Christ (i.e., the Roman Catholic Church) impel toward Roman Catholic unity (cf. LG 8). The ecclesial communities of the Reformation cannot be called churches in the proper sense of the term "church" because they are lacking the sacrament of orders and therefore they have not retained the authentic and full reality of the eucharistic mystery.

248. The ecumenical goal of these documents is not the *communio ecclesiarum.* It is — however you look at it — either the return to the Roman Catholic Church's unity or the future entry into it. Only a strict further development of the ecclesiology of *communio* toward a real *communio ecclesiarum* — the beginnings of which one can find in LG and in UR — will be able to overcome the Rome-centered ecclesiology, which ends in an ecumenical impasse and makes every ecumenical dialogue about the unity of the church meaningless.

249. That the documents of the Congregation for the Doctrine of the Faith do not recognize the churches of the Reformation as churches in the proper sense has to do with the Roman Catholic nonrecognition of the ministry of the churches of the Reformation as a ministry in apostolic succession. But Alois Grillmeier had already pointed out in 1966, in his commentary to LG 15, that "insofar as participation in the ecclesial character instituted by Christ is conceded, this also implies recognition of the existence of Church authority or power to direct and govern."[30] Grillmeier here recalls the conciliar terminology of *separated churches and ecclesial communities.* The Council did not say which non-Roman churches can be called *church,* and which churches should be called *ecclesial communities.* Vatican II consciously left this question open. This would indicate that the Council wanted to take into account the self-understanding of the different churches.

250. For the Orthodox theology the following viewpoint holds:

The recognition of the ministry of a church as a true ministry depends on the recognition of the community in which this ministry is exercised, and

30. In *LThK,* Erg.-Bd. I (Freiburg, Basel, Vienna: Herder, 1966), p. 202. ET: *Commentary on the Documents of Vatican II,* vol. 1 (New York: Herder & Herder, 1967), p. 179.

not vice versa. . . . The Eucharist of the community gathered in the Holy Spirit around its bishop is the natural context of all . . . the ministries of the church, and it [the Eucharist] is not a by-product of the ministry [*Amt*], as is often maintained in the discussions about the ordained ministry.[31]

251. The ecumenical upshot of this viewpoint is that the apostolicity of the church is constituted by the apostolic faith, which is confessed in common by the different Christian churches (Holy Scripture and the Creed of A.D. 381), and not by the historic apostolic succession of the bishops, supposedly unbroken since the time of the apostles. The ancient church episcopal ministry *expresses* the apostolicity of the church, but it does not *constitute* it.

2. Lutheranism and the Catholicity of the Church

252. Although Lutheran churches from the very beginning did not cease to emphasize and confess the catholicity of the church, their historical development in different regions displayed a tendency to territoriality and particularity (see above, Chapter III.A). This sometimes resulted in an ecclesial provincialism that confused the boundaries of the church with those of the *national* church and, accordingly, lost sight of the more comprehensive communion of the universal church.

253. Not surprisingly, such territorial narrow-mindedness has considerably weakened the sense of the unity of *ecclesia catholica* and has on occasion even made efforts toward church unity appear next to meaningless. What other church communions teach seems to be of little practical interest for the territorial church and can therefore hardly be applied as a benchmark or correction for its own doctrinal or any other activity. The territorial church is prior to the church universal, which, therefore, can only claim attention as long as the relationship between the universal and territorial church remains without conflict. In case of dispute, however, possible corrections, be they from world Lutheranism or from the wider Oecumene, are likely to be ignored and belittled or met by more or less blunt repudiations.

254. This also explains why the efforts of the Lutheran World Federation to use the federation as a platform for creating a Lutheran *communio* have

---

31. Anastasios Kallis, "Um den Bischof im Heiligen Geist versammelte Gemeinde: Der Bischof in der Tradition der orthodoxen Kirche," in *Bischofsamt: Amt der Einheit*, ed. Wilm Sanders (Munich: Pfeiffer, 1983), p. 61.

succeeded only recently and so far only partially, and why in the major Lutheran churches a universal Lutheran primacy of whatever kind remains disputed and contested. One can cite in this connection the often fruitless and only by exception successful attempts to proclaim a *status confessionis,* so as to activate the *munus propheticum ecclesiae* under difficult and acute circumstances. The autonomy and individuality of Lutheran territorial and national churches can often hinder them from adequately carrying out in their life what the vital rootedness in the tradition of the church universal would demand, with her responsibility to Scripture and to the creeds of the early church. Such traits weaken the energy of the faith's catholicity, which is so important for being Christian and for being church.

255. In such a situation, the unity of the church loses all concreteness and bearing on church life, and is shifted to the invisible connection with Christ. The very idea of a primatial institution with the task of ensuring church unity can even be misunderstood as an arrogant and damnable attempt to replace by human efforts, and hence to violate, the unity already given in Christ. Thus in several Lutheran churches one arrives at the conclusion, a conclusion that is, to say the least, ecumenically surprising, that efforts to concretize ecclesial unity are ill-conceived and mistaken, a result of misunderstanding. Here unity becomes totally spiritualized, which provides a platform for arguing that all efforts to establish a visible unity of the church as well as all claims of primacy are at best superfluous and at worst expressions of human and ecclesial abuse of power.

256. This attitude quickly and easily develops an atmosphere of prejudices and mistrust over against all primatial measures of supervision as well as an indifference to the concern for ecclesial unity. Both are extremely detrimental to all efforts toward mutual understanding, not to speak of accepting a universal function of church unity. Under these circumstances, a renewed appreciation of the necessary dimension of the catholicity of the church has to be rediscovered and encouraged. Together with the recognition of the serious and threatened situation of the divided churches in a shrinking Christian world, this will no doubt be an indispensable prerequisite for many Lutherans to take seriously the 1995 ecumenical overture of John Paul II. Otherwise his step is likely to be taken as a renewed Roman attempt to bring non-Catholic churches to accept the papacy. The invitation by the pope to theologians of other churches to consider together with Catholic theologians a possible future shape of the Petrine ministry, however, should be seen as something other and more than that.

Ut unum sint: Toward a Renewal of the Petrine Ministry

257. The report presented here attempts to form a bridge between the Lutheran reservations with regard to the papal office or ministry and the understanding of the same in the Roman Catholic Church. The main pillars of this bridge are, on the one hand, an analysis of the judgments of Luther and the Lutheran Reformation regarding the papacy and, on the other, that of the doctrine of the First and Second Vatican Councils. The renewed understanding of the church at Vatican II as *communio ecclesiarum* functions as the connecting span between the two. Upon this basis there result, from the Lutheran as from the Catholic side, perspectives for a convergence as well as queries about the present form and practice of the papal primacy. There then follows a survey of developments, both promising and problematical, that have taken place to date in ecumenical dialogues and in magisterial pronouncements.

258. Since the two papal dogmas of Vatican I have proven to be a decisive obstacle blocking convergence right up to the present, some further points by way of conclusion are in order. These are perspectives that derive from the present-day interpretation of the two dogmas as based on recent historical research and in light of the *communio* ecclesiology of Vatican II.

A. Hermeneutical Principles for the Rereading of Vatican I (Summary)

259. The results of newer historical investigations allow one now in fact to distinguish the actually intended meaning of Vatican I from the way it was expressed under the circumstances prevailing at that time. It was this garb,

however, this way of formulating the doctrine, that favored the prevailing maximalist interpretation of both dogmas in the past. That Council had no intention of either denying or rejecting the tradition of the first millennium, to wit: the church as network of mutually communicating churches. Although it may certainly be premature to state that the divergences concerning the papal ministry have been overcome, the new view of Vatican I allows Lutherans and others to arrive at a new assessment of the conciliar definitions.[1]

260. The achievements of other dialogues, especially those of the Orthodox-Catholic dialogue on primacy and jurisdiction,[2] could have important implications for the Lutheran-Catholic deliberations on papacy, especially if one adopts a new reading and interpretation of Vatican I in light of previous councils and Vatican II. In this context, some speak of the need for a rereading,[3]

1. Long since prepared and developed by Klaus Schatz and Hermann Josef Pottmeyer in their basic research on Vatican I, see above, Ch. II, note 1.

2. As an example of the possible rereading and re-reception, see the statement of the Joint International Commission for the Theological Dialogue between the Catholic Church and the Orthodox Church, "Ecclesiological and Canonical Consequences of the Sacramental Nature of the Church: Ecclesial Communion, Conciliarity, and Authority," Ravenna, October 15, 2007, *The Ecumenical Review* 60 (2008): 319-33. See especially paragraphs 18-44.

3. For example Joseph Ratzinger: "Just as within Holy Scripture there is the phenomenon of *relecture,* of the interpretive repetition of old texts in a new situation, whereby the former is newly understood, but the new is also connected back into the unity with the former, so likewise the individual dogmas and pronouncements of the Councils are not to be understood as isolated, but rather in the process of dogmatic-historical relecture within this unity of the history of faith. The new text is to be read in unity with the previous ones, as these are conversely brought into the present and developed by means of the new. That this insight is of fundamental significance for the interpretation of Vatican I is obvious . . . (Joseph Ratzinger, *Das neue Volk Gottes: Entwürfe zur Ekklesiologie,* 2nd ed. [Düsseldorf: Patmos, 1970], pp. 140-41). In this text, two aspects get overlooked: 1. The entire *post-apostolic* churchly doctrinal tradition of the history of dogma, from its beginnings till now, is subject to the criterion of the content of Holy Scripture; it is always to be understood in line with the *apostolic* witness of Scripture, whence the doctrine remains subject to correction. In this respect a relecture in the history of dogma cannot simply without qualification be compared to an inner-biblical relecture or put on the same level with it. That would necessarily be equivalent to regarding all post-apostolic doctrine in the church teaching of any given time (by reason of the thoroughgoing unity of the history of faith, as claimed) as representing the revealed truth in the contemporary age and developing it anew, all without the possibility of verification. Not even in the Counter-Reformation theory of the two sources of divine revelation does such a claim arise. 2. Another aspect overlooked in this idealistic presentation of the "unity of faith" or of believing is the oft-repeated phenomenon of breaks, losses, and even deviations, which have again and again been the occasion for reform and renewal movements. Here a reference to LG 8.3 is called for: "Ecclesia . . . sancta simul et semper purificanda poenitentiam et renovationem continuo prosequitur."

while others speak about the urgency of a re-reception of the First Vatican Council.[4]

> According to the Catholic view, such a re-reception does not put into question the validity of the definitions of the Council, but concerns its interpretations. For reception does not mean an automatic merely passive acceptance, but a lively and creative progress of appropriation.[5]

261. A rereading of the Vatican texts is not only an issue for theological scholarship, but appears to be practiced in the very center of the Roman Catholic Church. This fact is in line with the ecumenical encyclical of John Paul II and allows for a fresh understanding of the Vatican decisions of 1870 with far-reaching consequences for the interpretation of primacy and infallibility.

262. The new hermeneutic approach emphasizes the importance of not interpreting the dogma on the Petrine ministry in isolation, but in connection with the general ecclesiology of *communio* and in the light of the gospel and the whole tradition as well as in its historical context of the nineteenth century.[6] This leads to a concept of *papal primacy* as a *primatus communionis ecclesiarum* with some very important implications: the unity of the *ecclesia una* does not exclude a plurality and diversity of *ecclesiae*. Papal primacy, therefore, neither implies centralization nor uniformity, neither absorption nor fusion of churches.[7] Does such an approach to the issue of *primatus* open the way for

4. For example Yves Congar, *Diversités et communion: Dossier historique et conclusion théologique* (Paris: Éditions du Cerf, 1982).

5. Walter Kasper, "Petrine Ministry and Synodality," *The Jurist* 66, no. 1 (2006): 302. The concept of reception is fundamental for the ecumenical theology: cf. Yves Congar, "La réception comme réalité ecclésiologique," *RSPhTh* 56 (1972): 369-403; Alois Grillmeier, "Konzil und Rezeption," in Alois Grillmeier, *Mit ihm und in ihm: Christologische Forschungen und Perspektiven* (Freiburg, Basel, Vienna: Herder, 1975), pp. 309-34; Wolfgang Beinert, "Die Rezeption und ihre Bedeutung in Leben und Lehre," in *Verbindliches Zeugnis*, vol. 2: *Schriftauslegung, Lehramt, Rezeption*, Dialog der Kirchen 9, ed. Wolfhart Pannenberg and Theodor Schneider (Freiburg, Basel, Vienna: Herder; Göttingen: Vandenhoeck & Ruprecht, 1995), pp. 193-218; Gilles Routhier, *La réception d'un concile*, Cogitatio fidei (Paris: Éditions du Cerf, 1993), p. 174.

6. Walter Kasper, "Relire Vatican I: Une tâche oecuménique prioritaire pour l'Église catholique," *Istina* 50 (2005): 341-52.

7. The considerations of Joseph Ratzinger (see note 3 above), *Das neue Volk Gottes*, p. 142, point in a similar direction: "Only the faith is indivisible; the unitive function of the primacy is ordered to the faith. Everything else can and may be distinct and hence is open to autonomous governing functions, as they were realized in the ancient church in the 'primates' or patriarchates: unity of the church need . . . not mean unitary church [*Kircheneinheit muss . . . nicht Einheitskirche bedeuten*]. Consequently one should regard it as a task for the future to

"a unique form of Reformation Christianity in the unity of the one church"[8] as an *Ecclesia Lutherana Catholica?* This by no means implies a uniatism: "'uniatism' can no longer be accepted either as a method to be followed nor as a model of the unity our churches are seeking."[9]

263. Concerning *papal infallibility* the rereading of the Vatican texts also offers some important corrections that do away with many a prejudice and customary misunderstanding:

- the infallibility of the pope is no personal quality, his *infallibilitas* pertaining only to quite extraordinary undertakings, in which he appears as supreme teacher of the church in matters of *fides et mores* with an ultimately binding claim;
- *infallibilitas papae* can not be separated from the *indefectibilitas ecclesiae.* Parallel to the institution of the *status confessionis,* infallibility serves the authentic formulation of ultimately binding definitions of truth. Among Lutherans and Catholics it is not controversial that authoritative teaching is necessary, but the way in which this is actually done, is so far highly disputed. The Catholic Church responds to that challenge through the infallible teaching ministry, the Lutherans — though not disposing of institutionalized and theoretically sufficiently based instruments to do so — by means of declaring a *status confessionis.*[10] Thus both confessions,

---

distinguish more clearly the specific responsibility [*das eigentliche*] of the successor of Peter from [his] patriarchal ministry [*das patriarchale*]. Where needed, one should create new patriarchates and take them out of the Latin church. Accepting unity with the pope would no longer mean being integrated into a united administration. It would mean solely insertion into the unity of faith and, while according to the pope the power of binding interpretation, when that takes place in definitive form."

8. Ratzinger, *Das neue Volk Gottes*, p. 143.

9. "Uniatism: Method of Union of the Past, and the Present Search for Full Communion," Roman Catholic-Orthodox Joint International Commission, Balamand, Lebanon, 23 June 1993, no. 12, *GiA* II, 681.

10. The Lutheran churches trust that the teaching service in them and between them is fulfilled in cooperation between many different persons, authorities, and processes. They know that they must hope in, and pray to, the Holy Spirit to preserve the churches in the truth. However, if this trust in the Holy Spirit is not to be misconceived spiritualistically, and if it is acknowledged that the Holy Spirit takes people and institutions into his service to do his work, then the Lutheran Church cannot and must not withdraw from the task of teaching and decision-making that transcends the individual churches. It is also obvious that they can only get involved in processes of common formation of doctrine if it is clear that an openness to the witness of Holy Scripture exists in them and if their confessional tradition is taken seriously. The analogous question and challenge are especially posed to the teaching office of the

although differently and with different weight, teach authoritatively and give concrete shape to their Christian faith over against the world *(munus propheticum ecclesiae);*

- the infallibility is not unconditional: the pope is only infallible when acting explicitly as supreme teacher of the church, with the intention to commit the church universal to the truth now to be defined, in adherence to the revelation given once for all in Christ and witnessed in Holy Scripture.

264. Concerning *papal jurisdiction* (described by Vatican I as ordinary and immediate) the rereading of the Vatican texts likewise provides possibilities for overcoming prejudices and common misunderstandings:

- the Catholic tradition distinguishes ordinary from delegated power, the former being the power that pertains to a person by virtue of his specific charge, the latter, however, the power being exercised on behalf of another person. In this sense the power of the pope is ordinary, and Vatican I does not make the pope a bishop of the individual dioceses;
- the power of the pope is immediate, i.e., it can be exercised without recourse to an intermediary;
- on the other hand, since papal power is limited in various ways, the pope is no absolute monarch:
  1. the same fullness of power pertains to the bishops assembled in a council together with the pope. Episcopal power does not derive from the power of the pope, nor does this power infringe on the rights of a council;
  2. papal jurisdiction is limited by natural and divine law as well as normally by canon and customary law, and the pope is bound to revelation and conciliar decisions and must respect the fundamental church constitution, including the episcopate and thus the dioceses as well as conciliar and collegial order.
  3. while papal authority according to Vatican I is "ordinary" and "imme-

---

Bishop of Rome and that of the College of Roman Catholic Bishops. How should they understand, and how realize, a *universal* teaching ministry in such a way that it would take the teaching traditions of other Christian churches as seriously as their own? Without such a commitment, one can hardly speak of a *universal* teaching office worthy of the name, nor can churches other than the Roman Catholic Church be expected to recognize the true voice of the gospel in the declarations of this teaching ministry.

diate," the pope does not normally interfere in the day-to-day life of
the local church, but only by exception and in cases of emergency;
4. papal jurisdiction is always bound to promote the edification of the
church and never to imperil its divine law and order.

B. Conclusions and Implications

265. Based upon recent theological and ecumenical developments and particularly in the light of important results gained from the new hermeneutical
approach as described above, the Farfa Sabina Group notes that a new situation
is taking shape, in which revised assessments become possible that pave the
way to a common understanding of a ministry of universal ecclesial unity.

1. New Assessments

1.1. New Evaluation of the Papal Ministry by the Lutheran Churches

266. In this light papacy has lost its character as a necessarily invincible controversial issue between Lutherans and Catholics. If Vatican I is interpreted as
shown above, Lutherans may be prepared to acknowledge papacy as a legitimate expression of the Petrine ministry of unity for the Roman Catholic
Church. This does not mean that the present form of the papal office is regarded by the Lutheran churches as appropriately embodying the universal
ecclesial ministry of unity for the *communio ecclesiarum* of the future.

1.2. The Roman Catholic Church and the communio ecclesiarum

267. A key inference of the *relecture* of the decrees of Vatican I in the light of
Vatican II and in the light of the ecclesial reality of the first millennium is that
church unity is to be understood as *communio ecclesiarum*. A *communio ecclesiarum* presumes, however, that the ecclesiality of the bodies that are to form
this communion should not be in question. This requires on the Catholic side
the recognition of the Lutheran churches as churches,[11] and conversely on the

---

11. Such a recognition could take its orientation from the "Joint Declaration on the Doctrine of Justification" solemnly signed on October 31, 1999, in Augsburg by the Catholic Church
and the Lutheran World Federation (along with the "Annex" and the "Official Common State-

Lutheran side, recognizing that the shape of the Catholic Church is not contrary to the gospel. Again, this does not mean that the different churches have to acquiesce in the features that characterize the other church. But each church has to mutually acknowledge that what makes a church a church is present in the other. The Catholic understanding of the church as *communio ecclesiarum* is in principle open to the recognition of various embodiments of the church of Jesus Christ. This possibility implies as well an openness for other church-governing ministries, including the papal ministry.[12]

1.3. Consequences

268. In the case that the twin presuppositions are fulfilled, then a unity in reconciled diversity is possible. Given a reorientation of this nature, a papal office could develop with the charge of serving the unity of all churches. Our dialogue has shown that the controversial issues are by no means insurmountable. The mutual reassessments reveal a new perspective, one that does not mean the continuation of the current status quo, but that opens the gates to a Petrine ministry on a shared understanding.

2. On the Way to a Common Understanding of the Petrine Ministry

2.1. Petrine Ministry and Council

269. In the Roman Catholic Church, the highest level of the magisterium resides in the pope — and in the bishops together with the pope, either convened in council or dispersed over the whole globe. In view of our dialogue, a proposal in the interest of ecumenism follows: namely, that the pope might declare that he and his successors would in future normally make dogmatic decisions only after a broad public discussion, and in cooperation with the bishops, the representatives of other churches, and after having consulted experts in the field in question, as would be in conformity with the predominant church tradition. The classic and most appropriate place for such consultation would

---

ment," http://www.vatican.va/roman_curia/pontifcal_coun-cils/chrstuni/documents/rc_pc_chrstuni_doc_31101999_cath-luth-official-statement_en.html), which explicitly confirms that the churches have remained in the truth of the gospel and of the apostolic faith.

12. See the dogmatic correction made in LG 28, where only the ecclesiastical ministry as such is said to be "divinitus institutum," but not its threefold pattern of orders, which was defined by the Council of Trent as "divina ordinatione instituta" (*ND* 1719; *DH* 1776).

be a council.[13] The conciliar option corresponds to the example of the early church, the demands of the Reformation and of the Fourth General Assembly of the World Council of Churches in Uppsala 1968, and the concept subsequently developed in the ecumenical movement of church unity as conciliar fellowship.

270. This idea of a council poses a challenge for both the churches of the Reformation and the Roman Catholic Church. Adverting to it could give the reality of catholicity and universality more prominence in the awareness of the Lutheran churches.[14] In Roman Catholicism, it would be the spur to implement synodality and participation of the laity (church as People of God) at all levels of church life.

13. Primacy and conciliarity do not exclude each other. Within the Latin church of the West, the popes feared the loss of their power if they accepted the late medieval conciliarism that had ended the Western schism. Rome likewise declined to deal with the controversies of the early Reformation through a free council. When the Council of Trent was finally convened, much too late, it was seen in the eyes of many contemporaries and the following generations more as a papal event than as a council. During the Counter-Reformation and the following periods, the conciliar element was marginalized within the life of the Roman Catholic Church, and at the same time the image of the church was focused on the primacy of the pope and on clerical hierarchy. More and more the idea of conciliarity disappeared from the consciousness of the Roman Catholic faithful. — In striking contrast to this Roman Catholic trend, the conciliar or synodal element is what shapes the life of the churches of the Reformation and of the Orthodox churches. It plays a dominant and decisive role in the structuring of the whole of church life. Especially within the Orthodox churches, the Patriarch and his synod or the bishops and their synods are dependent on one another; both of them are responsible in common for authoritative leadership within the church. Emblematic of this contrast are the signatures put to ecumenical documents. The mutual excommunication of the eleventh century between Rome and Constantinople was revoked in 1965 by both sides; the common declaration was signed by "Pope Paul VI" and by "Patriarch Athenagoras I together with his synod" (see DwÜ I, 522f.; also www.vatican.va/holy_father/paul_vi/ speeches/1965/documents/hf_p-vi_spe_19651207_common-declaration_en). — At Vatican Council II the Roman Catholic Church rediscovered the conciliar element in its importance for the life of the church. This element was to be strengthened and upgraded by the introduction of councils, at first merely consultative. On all levels of the church (local, regional, universal) councils were established: parish councils, diocesan councils, national conferences of bishops, etc. But these councils remained only consultative. At the universal level Vatican II wanted to strengthen the importance of the synod of bishops with regard to the government of the church. To date, however, no decisive role has been accorded to any of these councils. This is also the case with the synod of the bishops. A truly synodal relationship of the primate to the college of bishops has not really developed in the Roman Catholic Church, although it is urgently needed today.

14. See above, Chapter IV.B.2.

2.2. *Ministry of Unity and Pastoral Leadership or Oversight*

271. *Episkopē* (office of overseer, 1 Tim. 3:1) is of the essence of the church. In our churches, it is carried out personally, collegially, and/or synodally. Different ministries attend to *episkopē* in the individual churches: in the Roman Catholic Church, it is the office of bishops; in the Lutheran churches, there is an interplay of official persons (bishops, church presidents, etc.) and synods. Concerning the biblical notion of *episkopein* and episcopal succession and the apostolic continuity of the church, there is much agreement that apostolic succession and apostolic continuity need to be articulated together and never taken without reference to the other dimension. The bishop is, therefore, never to be seen as an individual detached from a community of believers. This applies also to the Bishop of Rome. Ancient tradition accords him an honorary preeminence among the bishops, while at the same time he is a member of the college of bishops *as pastor of his community.* A future occupant of the office of universal ecclesiastical unity would have great responsibilities, to the extent that the churches can commit themselves to such an office. It would be within his power to convene a council and incumbent upon him to care for the unity of the churches and attend to the pastoral needs of all believers (pastoral ministry). In consultation with and voting by the churches, he would determine when it is necessary to decide, to teach, and to worship in common, and what may legitimately be left to local communities to decide, teach, and how to worship. Decisions at the level of the universal church, after all, are often not the best solutions for problems at the regional and local levels. Regional and local synods can often handle their own problems satisfactorily. Thus synodality and collaboration are called for at and between all levels: local, regional, and universal — all the more so in a world that is becoming more and more globalized while at the same time emphasizing regional identities.

2.3. *Petrine Ministry in Service of Truth*

272. As stated above, the divine promise to abide in the truth is primarily to be understood as connected with the *indefectibilitas ecclesiae.* The promise is given to the church of Christ as such. The ecclesial authority is only acting as the church's authentic witness when defining the truth and guiding the faithful. This implies that decisions of councils and papal actions are always in need of reception on the part of the people of God in order to become what they are meant to be: expressions of the church's abiding in the truth and of the tireless struggle to comprehend it in view of the uncounted challenges that face the

churches. In this situation the lack of a ministry entrusted with the ecumenical agreement of Lutheran churches is an especially grievous ill.

273. The Vatican I dogma is not in opposition to the development of synods at all levels of the Catholic Church nor to the reception of doctrinal pronouncements by the People of God as a whole. All this stands in line with the reference made by Vatican I to the old tradition of the church as arriving at the truth — as well as with the explanations of the commissions reporting to the Council, which emphasized the principle of the need for appropriate consultation and the subsidiary character of *ex cathedra* definitions.

274. The Second Vatican Council underlines this at several important junctures in its teaching: on the bishops' college and its co-responsibility for the good of the whole church, on the active participation of the laity in the faith life of the church, and on the character of the church as *communio ecclesiarum*. The Council similarly validates the testimony to the faith contributed by the particular churches in the way of partnership and collegiality in arriving at the truth and making decisions. The 1998 study of the Congregation for the Doctrine of the Faith, *The Primacy of the Successor of Peter in the Mystery of the Church,* aptly states:

> Listening to what the Churches are saying is, in fact, an earmark of the ministry of unity, a consequence also of the unity of the Episcopal Body and of the *sensus fidei* of the entire People of God. . . . The ultimate and absolute responsibility of the Pope is best guaranteed, on the one hand, by its relationship to Tradition and fraternal communion and, on the other, by trust in the assistance of the Holy Spirit who governs the Church.[15]

275. In an ecumenical perspective, such a declaration by Rome on the future conduct of the popes would be a step toward reaching an understanding. This step would also correspond to the willingness expressed by Pope John Paul II in his encyclical letter *Ut unum sint* to take ecumenical concerns into account in the way he exercises his ministry. A further contribution to this ecumenical concern could also take the form of extending the consultation prior to dogmatic doctrinal decisions to the non-Catholic churches and communities, as already happened at the Second Vatican Council with the invitation and cooperation of non-Catholic observers.

276. If the communion of the churches is the horizon of the ministry of

---

15. See www.doctrinafidei.va/documents/rc_con_cfaith_doc_19981031_primato-successore-pietro_en.html#top. Cf. above, note 6 in the introduction, and note 19 of Chapter III.

universal church unity, and if this ministry is exercised within this framework, then the churches — "together, of course," as John Paul II put it — can discover the advantages of such a ministry. It will have to be exercised *communi consensu* (UR 14). Free from the fetters of received ways, a completely new form of Petrine ministry can be sought, together with the other churches, in and for the *communio ecclesiarum.* If the holder of this ministry of universal church unity should one day turn to all Christians and to the bishops and guides of other churches, he could speak like Peter in the spirit of the First Letter of Peter:

> Now as an elder myself and a witness of the sufferings of Christ, as well as one who shares in the glory to be revealed, I exhort the elders among you to tend the flock of God that is in your charge, exercising the oversight, not under compulsion but willingly, as God would have you do it — not for sordid gain but eagerly. Do not lord it over those in your charge, but be examples to the flock. (1 Pet. 5:1-3; NRSV)

Members of the Group of Farfa Sabina

Lutheran Members

Professor Torleiv Austad, Oslo, Norway
Professor André Birmelé, Strasbourg, France
Professor Sven-Erik Brodd, Uppsala, Sweden
Professor Theodor Dieter, Strasbourg, France
Professor Hans Gammeltoft-Hansen, Copenhagen, Denmark
Professor Harding Meyer, Strasbourg, France
Professor Peder Nørgaard-Højen, Copenhagen, Denmark (Lutheran Chairman)

Catholic Members

Professor Elena Bosetti, Modena, Italy
Professor Johannes Brosseder, Cologne, Germany
Professor Werner Jeanrond, Lund, Sweden (2nd session only)
Professor Hervé Legrand OP, Paris, France
Professor Hermann J. Pottmeyer, Bochum, Germany
Professor James F. Puglisi SA, Rome, Italy (Catholic Chairman)
Professor Teresa Francesca Rossi, Rome, Italy
Professor Myriam Wijlens, Erfurt, Germany

Secretariate

Bente Guldsborg, M.Th., Copenhagen, Denmark

Sessions
1. Farfa/Sabina: November 3-7, 2005
2. Camaldoli/Napoli: November 2-5, 2006
3. Farfa/Sabina: October 31–November 4, 2007
4. Farfa/Sabina: October 29–November 2, 2008
5. Farfa/Sabina: May 4-6, 2009
6. Farfa/Sabina: November 2-4, 2009

Editorial Group
Professor Johannes Brosseder
Professor Theodor Dieter
Professor Peder Nørgaard-Højen
Professor Hermann J. Pottmeyer
Bente Guldsborg, M.Th.
Venue: Birgittenkloster, Bremen/Germany

Editorial Group with regard to the English translation
Professor Johannes Brosseder
Professor Peder Nørgaard-Højen
Bente Guldsborg, M.Th.
Venue: Birgitta-klosteret, Maribo/Denmark